To

....

From

....

On this date

....

Print ISBN 978-1-62836-872-7

eBook Editions:
Adobe Digital Edition (.epub) 978-1-63058-598-3
Kindle and MobiPocket Edition (.prc) 978-1-63058-599-0

Published by Barbour Books, an imprint of Barbour Publishing, Inc., P.O. Box 719, Uhrichsville, Ohio 44683, www.barbourbooks.com

Our mission is to publish and distribute inspirational products offering exceptional value and biblical encouragement to the masses.

Member of the
Evangelical Christian
Publishers Association

Printed in the United States of America.

Inspiration for
Your Soul

This
Christmas,
God Wants You
To Know...

SHANNA D. GREGOR

BARBOUR BOOKS
An Imprint of Barbour Publishing, Inc.

INTRODUCTION

This Christmas, God has a special message—just for you! *This Christmas, God Wants You to Know. . .* will infuse your soul with the encouragement and inspiration you need to face the busy holiday season.

With each turn of the page, this beautifully designed devotional will delight and cheer you on in your daily faith walk, giving you insight into God's amazing love for you. Each heartwarming reading offers special reminders of just how much your heavenly Father cherishes you, not only at Christmas but all year long. Each inspirational thought is accompanied by a related scripture selection and refreshing devotional that will leave you feeling perfectly blessed. Listen for His still, small voice as you ponder these devotional readings.

This Christmas, God Wants You to Know. . .

He Sent His Greatest Gift Just for You

God has given us eternal life, and this life is in his Son.
1 John 5:11 niv

Each Christmas, no matter where the Anderson family went for Christmas, they opened at least one gift on Christmas Eve. But before a single gift was touched, the eldest in the house read the Christmas story, followed by a prayer.

This year was the first time in years that all nineteen children and grandchildren were able to travel to Grandpa and Grandma Anderson's house. As Grandpa picked up his Bible, everyone scurried to assemble, and a hush fell over the whole house as each one found a seat in the living room.

Four-year-old granddaughter Lizzy crawled under the Bible and into his lap, and she sat patiently until he finished. As he started to shut his Bible, Lizzy asked, "Grandpa, what was your best Christmas present?"

Expecting the older grandchildren to wiggle and squirm at the potential delay, he started to refuse, but children and grandchildren were listening intently—waiting to hear his answer. So, looking deeply into his youngest granddaughter's eyes, he said, "Of all the presents I ever received, the best gift ever was the one I received from God—when I asked Jesus to come into my heart, and He came and has never left."

Lizzy looked at her grandfather and said, "I want that to be my best present ever, too!"

---

*I pray this Christmas I will not lose sight that
You have given me the best present ever. Amen.*

This Christmas, God Wants You to Know. . .

HE WILL MEET ALL YOUR NEEDS

"For it was I, the LORD your God,
who rescued you from the land of Egypt.
Open your mouth wide, and I will fill it with good things."
PSALM 81:10 NLT

*B*rent had lost his job in August, and Hope would be on maternity leave for at least two months after the new baby arrived. Hope tried to push aside thoughts of what Christmas would be like without his income for the older two children. She prayed she could get the best price on a few groceries with the cash she had in her purse that day.

She marked the things she could get off her list, careful to add up what she was spending in her head, and estimated the tax. She got through the checkout line and dropped the two pennies she had left into the donation jar, thanking God she didn't go over.

She set her groceries into the car and started to shut the trunk when a young courtesy clerk called to her. "Ma'am, you have two more bags," he said.

"No, I only had these few bags. These two aren't mine."

He set the bags into her trunk and pointed. "That guy driving away told me to bring them to your car." Stunned, she peered into the bags to find the items still on her list. With tears of joy, she thanked God for meeting her needs once again.

Thank You for never allowing me to go without
but always providing what I need, Father. Amen.

This Christmas, God Wants You to Know. . .

THE COMFORT OF HIS PEACE

"My sheep listen to my voice; I know them, and they follow me.
I give them eternal life, and they will never die,
and no one can steal them out of my hand."

JOHN 10:27–28 NCV

The great American evangelist Billy Graham said, "Christ alone can bring lasting peace—peace with God—peace among men and nations—and peace within our hearts." Life can become so loud, you want to cover your ears and find a quiet place of peace to hide from the noise. As God's child, His peace lies within you. It is always with you, but sometimes you need to turn it up.

Think about the lullabies that quiet children when they are agitated, upset, or afraid. As the song plays, tears subside, and a calm pours into the room. Much like a soft, comforting song, God's peace can silence anxiety, confusion, fear, and stress. His peace flows through you, bringing a knowing that with God, all things are possible, and He holds your world in the palm of His hand.

This Christmas, listen for God's voice, and allow Him to bring security in the midst of whatever circumstance you're facing. Take comfort in His peace!

Lord, I look to You for comfort today.
I listen to Your voice and find comfort in Your presence
knowing You have filled me with Your peace. Amen.

This Christmas, God Wants You to Know. . .

THE BLESSING OF SERVING OTHERS

"And the King will answer them, 'Truly, I say to you,
as you did it to one of the least of these my brothers, you did it to me.' "
MATTHEW 25:40 ESV

*T*he choice to serve others can leave an impression in the hearts of that person and sometimes their families for generations to come. One man's decision to serve others is eloquently captured in a movie called *Schindler's List*. The final scene takes place at Oskar Schindler's grave as those he served placed stones on his grave. Even today there are small stones of all shapes and sizes placed respectfully one on top of the other on his gravesite.

Perhaps each stone placed is a promise made by the one who left it to remember something significant. Perhaps they are thanking God for one man's courage to stand up when it seemed no one else could. Maybe they owe their very lives to him because without him they would never have been born. Others may hope they have enough boldness for what they believe in when their time comes to stand.

Schindler chose to serve others and make a life-saving difference in their lives by doing what he could do. No matter how small your service to others may seem, God will use it to bring blessing to your life and to the lives of those you serve!

Thank You for the opportunity to serve others.
May I recognize the opportunities as they come and take action,
bringing blessing to their life and pleasure to You, God. Amen.

This Christmas, God Wants You to Know. . .

YOU CAN TRUST HIM TO KEEP EVERY PROMISE

"Therefore the Lord Himself will give you a sign: Behold, the virgin shall conceive and bear a Son, and shall call His name Immanuel."
ISAIAH 7:14 NKJV

*G*od always keeps His promises. In the Garden of Eden, God made a promise after Adam and Eve disobeyed God's only command—and ate of the tree in the center of the garden. Satan deceived Eve, which led to the promise that Christmas—the birth of the Messiah—would come. God said, "And I will cause hostility between you [Satan] and the woman, and between your offspring and her offspring. He will strike your head, and you will strike his heel."[1]

From that day in the garden, God reminded His people that He would deliver on His Christmas promise. In Deuteronomy 18:15, God says the Messiah will be a prophet like Moses. Isaiah heralded the coming of Christ a number of times during his life, including the declaration in Isaiah 7:14 foretelling Christ's conception and birth. Micah, Zechariah, Exodus, and the Psalms reveal details of the promise serving as reminders that lead to the delivery of the Christmas promise found in Luke 2. God made a Christmas promise, and two thousand years later, that promise was delivered.

Thank You for every promise You've made to me.
I trust You will deliver what You have promised right on
time—just as You delivered the Christmas promise
that gave me the gift of eternal life. Amen.

---

1 Genesis 3:15 NLT.

11

This Christmas, God Wants You to Know. . .

HE LOVES TO HEAR YOU PRAY

I love the LORD, because he has heard my voice and my pleas
for mercy. Because he inclined his ear to me,
therefore I will call on him as long as I live.
PSALM 116:1–2 ESV

*E*laina stood outside her daughter Tabitha's open bedroom door, watching her set out her things in preparation for the next school day. She could hardly believe she was already a teenager—growing up so fast.

Elaina turned to go to back to the kitchen and suddenly stopped when she heard Tabitha begin to pray. The words were so conversational. She had learned to talk to God anytime or anywhere, like she would her very best friend. She listened to her daughter's honest and open heart—words of adoration and praise poured from her lips.

For just a few moments longer, she listened and then returned to the kitchen. *I love hearing her pray,* she thought. She thought of her own prayer time with the Lord and how many times over the years her children had heard her pray. Then, deep within her heart she heard the Lord say, *I love to hear you pray even more than you enjoy hearing your child pray.* She suddenly felt like a little girl again, talking to her Father, God!

Lord, let my time with You bring me closer to You. Remind
me how much You love to hear from me, and never let me
forget how important our relationship is. Amen.

This Christmas, God Wants You to Know. . .

HE EXPECTS YOU TO SHARE THE GOOD NEWS

The angel said to them, "Do not be afraid. I am bringing you good news that will be a great joy to all the people. Today your Savior was born in the town of David. He is Christ, the Lord."
LUKE 2:10–11 NCV

*I*magine the magnificent display of majesty as a great congregation of angels woke your household with a burst of praise and an exclamation that God was born into the world as a baby, with a simple message—believe and live forever! The holiness of heaven came down and kissed the earth to celebrate God's promise fulfilled. God's plan to bring man back into relationship with Him was, by faith, already done!

When something wonderful happens, you share it. In this instant, God trusted men once again with a powerful secret. God was now flesh, in the earth. God's greatest desire was to return His gift of eternal life to His children. Once again, God would be a Father to all who would receive Him.

Visualize the shepherds' excitement. They went immediately to see the baby, Jesus. They shared with Mary and Joseph their experience.

Remember how you felt when you received Christ? Let the fire of God's greatest Christmas gift stir you once again. You hold that revelation in your heart, but God expects you to share the Good News with everyone.

Stir Your gift within my heart today. Like those who heard the angelic host of heaven worship and praise God—give me the courage to proclaim God's revelation to others. Amen.

This Christmas, God Wants You to Know. . .

He Will Always Answer You

"Call to Me, and I will answer you, and show you great and mighty things, which you do not know."
JEREMIAH 33:3 NKJV

Derek had found the set of club chairs his wife really wanted to put in the den at a consignment shop. They looked brand new. The lady selling them said they were rarely sat in because they belonged to her mother and she kept them in her formal living room—where they only entertained at Christmas. The problem was he needed another person to help him carry the big, overstuffed sectional out of the house before his wife got home from Christmas shopping.

He had texted and called several of his buddies, but the only one who replied was his brother-in-law, Matt, who was away on business, and he wouldn't be back in town until tomorrow. He went next door to his neighbors' houses, and no one answered the door. Several hours had passed, and he was growing concerned that his surprise would be ruined when another buddy finally returned his call and said he'd come over right then.

When you call on God, He is always there. He is ready to answer your prayers when you connect with Him. Although He knows your needs before you ask, He wants to hear from you. He desires a relationship with you.

Thank You for always being there when I call on You. I trust You for answers and the strength I need to face whatever challenge comes my way. Amen.

This Christmas, God Wants You to Know. . .

HE WILL NOT FAIL YOU

"No man shall be able to stand before you all the days of your life.
Just as I was with Moses, so I will be with you.
I will not leave you or forsake you."
JOSHUA 1:5 ESV

Alisha stood to the side of her new apartment building, allowing the movers to pass in front of her. Her hands were full of a box of precious things she had packed and brought with her in her own car—pictures of her family—the faces of those she had left behind just two days before. Now, she and her husband, Stewart, were on their own. Everything familiar was gone.

As she hugged her parents, her father leaned down and said, "Remember, God was with us when we moved here—He'll be there for you in your new place. Just listen for His direction and guidance and follow Him." Alisha remembered when her family moved to the small town she grew up in. Her mother had become very ill, and there was no one to call. God had sent an older lady from down the street to care for her mother, Alisha, and her sisters so her father could start his new job.

Over the next few months, Alisha reminded herself of the many times that God had been there for her family. His unfailing love gave her guidance and showed her the way.

God, You have never failed me,
and I know You never will. Amen.

This Christmas, God Wants You to Know. . .

THERE IS MORE TO HIM THAN THE MANGER

"There is no one like the God of Israel. He rides across the heavens to help you, across the skies in majestic splendor."
DEUTERONOMY 33:26 NLT

"Grandpa, what's a manger?" six-year-old Morgan asked as she watched her grandfather set the Nativity scene out on his lawn. Grandpa dropped the extension cords and motioned for Morgan to join him on the porch swing.

"When Jesus was born," Grandpa started, "His parents had traveled to another city. It was required that everyone come into the city at that time so the hotels were all full. There was no place for them to stay, so a kind person who owned a hotel let them stay in the barn. The stand that held the animals' food was called a manger and was probably about the size of your little brother's crib. It was the perfect place for baby Jesus to sleep His first night on earth."

Morgan nodded, and Grandpa continued. "We celebrate Christmas as a reminder that God came to earth as a baby, but it isn't just about a baby's birthday. God made a lot of promises to the people who love Him. One of those promises was that a child would be born who would save the world."

Choose this Christmas to spend some this season in holy wonder—considering with gratitude and worship all that God's love for you brings.

God, thank You for sending Jesus so I can experience Your promises in my life each day. Amen.

This Christmas, God Wants You to Know. . .

FATHER KNOWS BEST

*"The virgin will conceive and give birth to a son,
and they will call him Immanuel" (which means "God with us").*
MATTHEW 1:23 NIV

"Mary Did You Know," a song written by Mark Lowry and Buddy Green, quickly became a Christmas favorite as soon as it was released. It asks Mary, Jesus' mother, if she knew the wondrous things Jesus would do.

When the angel appeared to Mary and told her she had been chosen by God to deliver His Son to the world, she trusted God and said, "Let it be unto me." The appearance of an angel and the good news that God had chosen her was probably scary but very exciting. Looking back over Mary's life, there were great miracles but also great pain and sacrifice.

How many times have you wished you had not made a certain choice, even though you knew it was God leading you to do His will? If Mary had known that her son's life would be cut short, if she had known the tragedy and heartache she would experience as she watched Him be ridiculed, beaten, and hung on a cross to eventually die, would she have instead said, "Not me, God, choose someone else to bring Your Son into the world"?

*Heavenly Father, when the path You have placed me on brings
sacrifice and pain, give me the strength to hold on to You
and see it through, trusting that You know best! Amen.*

This Christmas, God Wants You to Know. . .

HE SUPPLIES GRACE FOR EVERY SEASON

"For I will pour water on him who is thirsty, and floods on the
dry ground; I will pour My Spirit on your descendants,
and My blessing on your offspring."
ISAIAH 44:3 NKJV

*I*t's just one thing after another with this house," Bridgett told her mother over the phone. "First the air conditioner went out, then the pool pump. Now that we finally have an offer on the house, they find termites and the first-time buyer is freaking out. I don't want to wait for another contract if they back out. Three months is too long for the boys and me to be living in one state and Ted in another."

"Oh, honey, I'm so sorry," her mother, Sonya, responded. "I know you're frustrated and you don't want to hear this, but God knows exactly when you guys need to go. He supplies grace for every season you go through." Bridgett let out an exasperated sigh, but her mother continued. "The wonderful thing about a difficult season is that eventually it will end. You will get through it. He's given you everything you need—every ounce of strength—to get to the next season."

"Thanks for reminding me that He never fails—and He will give me the grace to do what I need to do this time, too."

Father, I rely on Your grace today for all the strength I need
to get through the big ordeals and even the simple frustrations.
Amen.

This Christmas, God Wants You to Know. . .

IT'S ABOUT THE ONE

*"If a man has a hundred sheep and one of them gets lost,
what will he do? Won't he leave the ninety-nine others in the wilderness
and go to search for the one that is lost until he finds it?. . . In the
same way, there is more joy in heaven over one lost sinner
who repents and returns to God than over ninety-nine others
who are righteous and haven't strayed away!"*
LUKE 15:4, 7 NLT

Alicia noticed her five-year-old son in a panic, zipping through the kitchen into the living room, up the stairs, and back down again. He turned over the cushions in the couch, looked under the living room furniture, and then back into the kitchen.

"What are you looking for, Zane?" she asked him.

"My blue and white race car," he replied, now checking to see if it had slid under the refrigerator.

"Well, don't you have twenty-three other cars in that race set you got for Christmas?"

"Mom," he gasped, "that is the *one* car that is lost. I *have* to find it! It's about *that one*."

"Okay," Alicia said, trying to comfort him. She dried her hands on a towel and closed the dishwasher. "I'll help you look for it."

Just then, his sister called from upstairs, "I found it!" Zane rushed upstairs with a sigh of relief.

---

*Lord, thank You for being concerned about the one.
When I wander, You always come after me
and bring me safely back into Your presence. Amen.*

This Christmas, God Wants You to Know. . .

Your Faith Will Grow

But how can they call on him to save them unless
they believe in him? And how can they believe
in him if they have never heard about him?
And how can they hear about him unless someone tells them?

Romans 10:14 NLT

*E*ight-year-old Tommy asked Jesus into his heart but still had a question. The past few weeks he had overheard people talking about faith. He decided he needed to get some. He decided to ask his Uncle Pete about it. He figured he would know the answer.

"Uncle Pete," he began, after positioning himself onto the tailgate of his uncle's pickup truck, where he was working. "I got something 'portant to ask ya. How do people get faith?"

"Well," Pete replied, "you asked Jesus in your heart, and He came in, right?" Tommy nodded yes. "So you already have faith. You believed Jesus came into your heart with the faith you have. As you get to know Jesus better, you'll understand more about Him, like you get to know a friend."

"So faith is in me already?"

Uncle Pete nodded his head yes. "It's like when you eat healthy food that is good for you, your body gets what it needs for you grow strong and tall. When you learn more about God, then you give your faith what it needs to grow."

Lord, I believe in You. Help me to learn and grow
in my faith so I can know You more. Amen.

This Christmas, God Wants You to Know...

HE SEES THE REAL YOU

Where shall I go from your Spirit?
Or where shall I flee from your presence? If I ascend to heaven,
you are there! If I make my bed in Sheol, you are there!
PSALM 139:7–8 ESV

When you meet people, they ask what you do for a living, where you live, and what schools you went to. What clothing you wear in many arenas demonstrates your affluence and level of wealth. People worry about saying the right things to the right people to impress them.

Do you ever pretend everything is good when your heart is breaking inside? Maybe in order to keep from offending your family or your boss, you don't express the complete truth about a situation or circumstance.

God sees the real you. He looks directly into your heart. You can't pretend with Him. He sees you where you are today—with your disappointments and hurts—but He doesn't stop there. He also sees you from the future. He wants to give you a picture of who He created you to become so you can begin to see yourself—not as others look at you—but as He sees you.

You can be real with God. He's not going to condemn, criticize, or judge you. He accepts you where you are right now.

God, teach me who I am as a result of who
You created me to be. Show me how to use the gifts
and talents You have given to me for Your glory. Amen.

This Christmas, God Wants You to Know. . .

FAMILY IS HIS IDEA

The Word became flesh and made his dwelling among us.
We have seen his glory, the glory of the one and only Son,
who came from the Father, full of grace and truth.
JOHN 1:14 NIV

Hilary sat on the couch watching her children and grandchildren open their Christmas gifts. The sound of their voices faded away, and for a moment, she stepped back into time, remembering when her father would say to her and her two younger brothers: "Let's go get our Christmas tree."

"Mom. . .Mom," her daughter, Sherry, called. "What were you thinking about?"

"I was just remembering when I was a little girl how my daddy would take us to get our Christmas tree. My mother would help my brothers and me bundle up in snow boots, ski pants, hats, gloves, and scarves. Then we'd trudge across the meadow, through the deep snow, and into the woods to find our live tree. Dad would point out different ones, and we'd help him pick it out.

"He'd chop it down, and we'd drag it to the back porch and shake all the snow off it before setting it up in the house. I still think of those childhood Christmases in the country every time I smell pine. It reminds me of how important family is, especially at Christmas."

God created you to be a part of His family.

Thank You, God, for the opportunity to live my life
as a part of Your heavenly family. Amen.

This Christmas, God Wants You to Know. . .

WORSHIP BRINGS REST FOR YOUR SOUL

O LORD, You brought my soul up from the grave;
You have kept me alive, that I should not go down to the pit.
Sing praise to the LORD, you saints of His, and give thanks
at the remembrance of His holy name.

PSALM 30:3–4 NKJV

*E*xhausted, Sandy walked slowly into the church. She found a seat and waited for the service to start, lost in her thoughts. *What a week,* she thought. She leaned back a little in the seat and tried to relax.

She replayed the last few days over in her mind as her eighteen-year-old daughter, Alex, packed her car and drove fifteen hundred miles away. She was determined to live on her own. Sandy's heart was torn because she didn't believe Alex's decision was God's path for her life, but Alex was eighteen and there was no changing her mind.

The praise team encouraged the congregation to stand and join in worship. Sandy didn't feel like joining in, but she knew if she would just reach out to God, He would meet her more than halfway. She began to sing the words and opened her broken heart to Him.

She began to breathe in His healing presence, and she felt her soul gain strength. She accepted His love. She trusted Him with Alex's life. She felt His assurance that He would be there for Alex always.

Worship and praise are free therapy. Thank You for bringing peace through my praise to my wounded soul. Amen.

This Christmas, God Wants You to Know. . .

ONLY HE CAN SATISFY THE DESIRE IN YOUR SOUL

*My soul yearns for you in the night; my spirit within me earnestly
seeks you. For when your judgments are in the earth,
the inhabitants of the world learn righteousness.*

ISAIAH 26:9 ESV

One of the biggest challenges most people face each day
is that they are seldom satisfied. There is a healthy balance
required. It's necessary to set goals, dream, and look forward,
but the opportunity to get stuck exists when the focus is
on *getting* instead of on the Giver. It's dangerous to think a
particular something will fill a longing in the soul.

The belief that more money, a newer car, a better job, or
that perfect spouse will bring contentment is a misguided
focus. God had provided Adam and Eve with everything
they could have wanted, but they wanted the one thing
God said was forbidden! If only they had pursued God, and
the contentment that comes from a relationship with Him,
things could have turned out differently.

Christmas isn't just about exchanging gifts but about
the gifts God has given. It is a season to reflect on what God
has done and to recognize that He must become the greatest
desire of your soul.

This season, ask yourself, "What blessings have I been
given?" and then ask yourself, "How can I cherish them and
show I am thankful for them?"

*Lord, I will count my blessings and reflect on the reality that
only You can satisfy me. Help me to focus on You today! Amen.*

This Christmas, God Wants You to Know. . .

THE CHRIST OF CHRISTMAS LIVES IN YOU

The Spirit of God, who raised Jesus from the dead, lives in you.
And just as God raised Christ Jesus from the dead, he will give life
to your mortal bodies by this same Spirit living within you.
ROMANS 8:11 NLT

As Misty drove to the quaint little tearoom for lunch with Linda, she thought about this beautiful woman, old enough to be her mother, who had taken her under her wing and encouraged her. In a time when everything seemed wrong in her life, Linda was there.

When she stepped into Linda's presence, it was as if no one else existed. She would become lost in conversation, hoping the time they had together would never end. She felt she could get through anything as long as Linda cheered her on. Her words were the encouragement she needed to get through each day. She found hope once again in her time with Linda.

The ladies said their good-byes, and Misty was alone with her thoughts. Suddenly she realized Linda could easily be mistaken for Christ. She lived her life so that others saw Christ in her. Misty became determined that day to set the bar to live her life for others in such a way that when they were in her presence, they saw Christ, too.

I commit to live my life in a way that
I might be mistaken for Christ.
Help me to be a reflection of You in all I say and do. Amen.

This Christmas, God Wants You to Know. . .

HE WILL GIVE YOU A FRESH PERSPECTIVE

The LORD will keep you from all evil; he will keep your life.
The LORD will keep your going out and your coming in
from this time forth and forevermore.
PSALM 121:7–8 ESV

After the birth of her third child, Cara immediately felt overwhelmed. Her mother had come to help the first few weeks. After she went back home, the months were swallowed up with furious activity of just keeping the kids clean, the house picked up, food on the table—and that was after a full day at work. Cara looked across the living room with the Christmas tree lights blinking their own quiet tune. The laundry basket piled with clean clothes was sat to the side. Her husband was in the recliner with the youngest on his chest, while the other two had fallen asleep on the ends of the couch.

She took a deep breath as God gently reminded her of His many blessings. In the chaos of all the laundry that never seemed to be done—her husband's military uniforms reminded her how thankful she was to have him home for the holidays when so many from their community were overseas. The socks, shoes, and toys that littered the house reminded her that her children were healthy and full of life. The empty plates, cups, pots, and pans gave her a fresh perspective that her family never went to bed hungry, cold, or feeling unloved.

Thank You for the reminders this Christmas that
I am blessed with heavenly abundance. Amen.

This Christmas, God Wants You to Know. . .

WISE MEN STILL WORSHIP HIM

When the wise men saw the star, they were filled with joy.
They came to the house where the child was and saw him with his
mother, Mary, and they bowed down and worshiped him. They opened
their gifts and gave him treasures of gold, frankincense, and myrrh.
MATTHEW 2:10–11 NCV

*T*ish straightened the product table that sat just outside the doors of the auditorium. She and a few other women were the only women at the men's worship event that had started about fifteen minutes ago. She tucked the bank bag under her arm and made for the kitchen for a cup of coffee. Her friend Amy met her there, and she poured another cup for her. "Let's go in and sit in the balcony. I know it's just for men, but the music sounds amazing."

The lights were dim and no one noticed as they made their way to the top tier of the balcony, since most of the men were seated on the floor and the middle tier of seats. The worship music seemed to pour over her and relax her tired body. Then she felt the strong and undeniable presence of the Lord.

Amy poked her and then pointed toward the floor. Thousands of men stood in reverence to God. She was excited to see God moving in the lives of these men who were willing to gather and worship Him.

Lord, I never want to miss an opportunity to worship You.
Amen.

This Christmas, God Wants You to Know. . .

JESUS CAME TO GIVE YOU ABUNDANT LIFE

"A thief comes to steal and kill and destroy,
but I came to give life—life in all its fullness."
JOHN 10:10 NCV

*T*ravis left a very difficult and stressful job. The only thing good about the job was the money—and it provided well for his family of four. The long hours and stress had affected his health, his family, and his marriage. It was time to do something different.

He had applied for other jobs within the company and tried to move to a new level, but he was so good at what he did, his boss feared he'd never find someone for that role, so after much prayer, he resigned his position and his wife, Patty, took up the slack by going back to work full-time.

He pressed to find another job, and his family was willing to move to a new location. Weeks of job hunting turned into months, but his health improved, his relationship with his children was stronger than ever, and he was finally spending time with God again. His trust in God's desire for his life grew stronger.

He realized his old job was a distraction that eventually would have stolen all the things that mattered most to him. Travis began to understand that his success was assured when he put God and His Word in first place.

I want to live the abundant life. I put Your Word in first place
in my life so that I can hear and follow You. Amen.

This Christmas, God Wants You to Know. . .

HE IS THE GREAT PROVIDER

And God is able to bless you abundantly, so that in all things at all times, having all that you need, you will abound in every good work.
2 CORINTHIANS 9:8 NIV

Growing up without a father, Angela saw her mother struggle most Christmases to put a single gift under the tree for her and her three younger sisters. When things were tight for them—not just at Christmastime—her mother would gather the four girls together for prayer. They would pray and ask God for whatever the need was: to repair the washing machine, to provide food or clothing, or to put gas in the car. Angela saw God provide for her most of her life.

As a young adult, the Lord opened doors and provided abundantly in every area of her life. Angela began to give back. Each year she found a different family, and she provided Christmas for them anonymously. It was her way to be the hands and feet of Jesus just as others had been for her and her family years ago.

Within the pages of the Bible, God demonstrates His faithfulness to satisfy the physical, emotional, and spiritual needs of His children. He is more than able to do "far more abundantly than all we ask or think."[2]

Thank You, Father, for Your promise to bless me in all things at all times. Thank You that I can come to You for whatever I need, and You are my Provider. Amen.

---

2 EPHESIANS 3:20 ESV.

This Christmas, God Wants You to Know. . .

He Believes in You

As it is written: "I have made you a father of many nations."
He is our father in the sight of God, in whom he believed—the God
who gives life to the dead and calls into being things that were not.
ROMANS 4:17 NIV

*I*f you have accepted Jesus as your Lord and Savior, then you are a child of the King, but the enemy of your soul wants you to believe nothing has changed. You are created in the image of God, and the more time you spend with Him—the more you get to know Him—the more like Him you become.

It's a process. In today's world, everyone wants things now. But God doesn't usually give you an overnight makeover. It takes time for the changes He's made in your heart to become realized in your mind, will, and emotions. He is working on you from the inside out.

Have faith and believe in Him; He believes in you. You were instantly made new in your spirit, redeemed, saved, and set free, but God is changing you. He's taking those things in your life that were hard, heavy, and burdensome and giving you freedom every day.

Trust the way He works in you. He has made you new. You are becoming something miraculous and stunning. He believes in you even when circumstances or people try to tell you otherwise.

Help me to believe in myself the way You do, Father. Amen.

This Christmas, God Wants You to Know. . .

A LITTLE CHANGE MAKES A BIG DIFFERENCE

To put off your old self, which belongs to your former manner of life and is corrupt through deceitful desires, and to be renewed in the spirit of your minds, and to put on the new self, created after the likeness of God in true righteousness and holiness.
EPHESIANS 4:22–24 ESV

Maggie and her teenage son, Carson, struggled to find common ground in their relationship with each new calendar year. Maggie pulled a box of Christmas ornaments from the garage into the living room. As she lifted each one out of the box, she was flooded with memories of Carson's childhood. She could almost hear the pitter-patter of his little feet across the floor as he ran to her, filling her face with slobbery, wet kisses as she lifted him into her arms.

Now his feet sounded like his father's—heavy and strong as he walked into the house. The words between them were few these days. Maggie knew the answer was to encourage and support in this season of her son's life—not to correct, pry, or tell him how to make decisions—but it was overwhelmingly difficult. He was so much like her, especially when she was his age. She wanted to spare him from the same mistakes, alleviating the hardships she had faced back them.

Lord, there are things I know I need to change in my life. Help me to stay committed to the change so I can see a difference in my own life and the lives of those I love. Amen.

This Christmas, God Wants You to Know. . .

HE HAS NOT FORGOTTEN YOU

But Jerusalem said, "The LORD has left me; the Lord has forgotten
me." The LORD answers, "Can a woman forget the baby she nurses?
Can she feel no kindness for the child to which she gave birth?
Even if she could forget her children, I will not forget you.
See, I have written your name on my hand."
ISAIAH 49:14–16 NCV

Ginger sat alone at the restaurant. Her friend Abigail was more than fifteen minutes late. She felt a little awkward sitting by herself, so she texted her friend to find out where she was. Minutes later, she received a text from Abigail. She had forgotten, and apologized, but was not going to make their lunch date. Ginger felt neglected, abandoned, and very silly for trusting that Abigail's busy schedule would not be a problem this time. Embarrassed, she slipped out of the restaurant quietly.

Christmas can sometimes be the loneliest of seasons. Standing alone and feeling isolated, or even in in the middle of a crowd of friends, you might feel like God has forgotten you. Challenges in life can sometimes make you feel like God is a million miles away. But unlike a friend who misses a lunch date, you can trust that God has not forgotten you!

Heavenly Father, I trust You to never leave me! You have written my name in the palm of Your hand. I will hold on to Your promise to always be with me. Amen.

This Christmas, God Wants You to Know. . .

HIS LIGHT WILL ALWAYS SHINE

In him was life, and that life was the light
of all mankind. The light shines in the darkness,
and the darkness has not overcome it.
JOHN 1:4–5 NIV

Jennifer and Jason had just purchased a new home weeks before Christmas. After a long day of unpacking, they decided to take their dog, Matty, for a walk and enjoy the neighborhood Christmas lights. Jason grabbed Matty's leash, and Jennifer found a flashlight they might need.

After passing about ten houses, Jennifer said, "Hey! I have not seen a single Nativity scene in the neighborhood." There were reindeer, snowmen, and plenty of Santa Claus representations but not a single representation of the Christ of Christmas in their neighborhood.

Back at the house, Jason asked Jennifer to follow him to the garage. He pulled out some two-by-fours and attached them in the formation of a cross. "What are you doing?" Jennifer asked. "I'm putting Christ in Christmas for our neighborhood. Here, help me," he told her.

Jennifer held the light as Jason dug a hole in the yard and positioned the cross in the hole. Then he wrapped all the white lights he could find around the cross. They stepped back into the street to admire the lights. It was simple, bright, and beautiful—and sent a powerful message.

I choose to let Your light shine into the lives
of others every day! Amen.

This Christmas, God Wants You to Know...

HIS TIME IS THE RIGHT TIME

*"For the vision is yet for an appointed time; but at the end it will
speak, and it will not lie. Though it tarries, wait for it;
because it will surely come, it will not tarry."*

HABAKKUK 2:3 NKJV

*L*eah's new job and her boss's personality challenged her
to take a second look at her strong desire to make a list and
"get it done." She discovered that some items had to wait. At
first her boss's relaxed management style frustrated her. Items
she felt needed his attention would sit on his desk for days.
As she observed his leadership style, she found that certain
things sat there for a reason. He seemed to be waiting—for
something.

Over the months, she lost count of the times she pressed
him because others were putting pressure on her to get the
job done. It didn't seem to bother him that a task sat idle on
her list and her phone rang repeatedly with people on the
other end waiting for his decision, which would also affect
their plan of action.

Eventually she learned to trust her boss's lead. Many
times something everyone felt was important turned out to
never have been a part of God's plan. Other times he would
press forward with clear direction and assurance.

*Lord, don't let me be impacted by what others think,
but teach me to follow Your instruction.
I want to do things in Your time. Amen.*

This Christmas, God Wants You to Know. . .

He Will Give You Rest

So there is a special rest still waiting for the people of God.
For all who have entered into God's rest have rested from
their labors, just as God did after creating the world.
Hebrews 4:9–10 nlt

"I am so overwhelmed," Kristie told her girlfriend Linda. "No matter how much I get done, I feel like I'm never going to catch up, and with added stress that comes with Christmas. . ."

Kristie took a breath. Linda let the silence hang in the air for a minute and then softly said, "I am your friend, and you know I'm going to tell you like it is."

A big sigh escaped Kristie's lips. Linda leaned over and put her hand on top of Kristie's. "When you put the Lord first, He will give you rest. He's promised that. Time with Him renews your soul and gives you strength to do the things He wants you to do."

"You're right," Kristie said, nodding her head in agreement. "I haven't been spending time with Him. That quiet time with the Lord gives me clarity to know what I need to do. It gives me the strength and a quiet peace in my heart. Thank you, Linda, for telling me the truth. I'm going to get alone with the Lord right now, and He'll show me how to reorder my day."

Lord, I need Your rest. I don't want to do things my way.
Help me to choose to live each day in Your rest. Amen.

This Christmas, God Wants You to Know. . .

ALL THINGS ARE POSSIBLE, IF ONLY YOU BELIEVE

Jesus looked at them intently and said, "Humanly speaking,
it is impossible. But not with God. Everything is possible with God."
MARK 10:27 NLT

Christmas is the biggest reality of God making the impossible, possible. What if the prophets who foretold of the Messiah had not spoken the promises of God to produce the seed of faith in the hearts of generations to come? What if Mary had not believed she would conceive the holy child without ever knowing a man? What if Joseph had not believed Mary had never been unfaithful in their relationship?

The faith to believe that God would do the impossible repeatedly brings Him onto the scene and into the lives of every generation. Hebrews 11 lists the names of those great men and women of faith who chose to believe God would do what He promised. Abel brought an acceptable offering to God by faith. Noah built a boat even though no one had ever seen rain, and he saved his family from the Great Flood. Abraham obeyed God and journeyed to a land he didn't know. He stepped out and started walking just because God told him to. Sarah gave birth to a child in her old age, after being unable to conceive in her youth.

What Christmas miracle does God want to do in you?

Sometimes I let doubt sneak in and steal my faith. Lord, help
me to believe that all things are possible today. Amen.

This Christmas, God Wants You to Know. . .

HE WANTS YOU TO DEPEND ON HIM

For God alone, O my soul, wait in silence, for my hope is from him.
He only is my rock and my salvation, my fortress;
I shall not be shaken. On God rests my salvation
and my glory; my mighty rock, my refuge is God.
PSALM 62:5–7 ESV

*A*lexis peeked into her seven-year-old son Jake's bedroom. Surprised, she found he had taken great care to straighten his bedroom in anticipation of their Christmas celebration with extended family that would arrive soon. She resisted the temptation to straighten the sheets hanging below the comforter.

"Excellent! Good job, Jake. You are really growing up and taking responsibility," she encouraged. He beamed and then hurried off, happy to have his chores done so he could go out and play with his brothers.

Alexis looked at the things in his bedroom. *He is growing up,* she thought. *He is more responsible—and much less dependent on me.* She was a little torn that he needed her less as he became more independent. She still liked feeling needed.

Her thoughts turned to her relationship with God. *Perhaps that is what surrender to God is like,* she thought. *He wants me to grow up and become who He intended me to be but also remain dependent on Him, willing to allow His influence to lead and guide me, while trusting that He is the support for my life that will always be there.*

God, I surrender to You. I depend on You to show
me your way of doing things. Amen.

This Christmas, God Wants You to Know...

His Example Is the Best One to Follow

*Follow God's example, therefore, as dearly loved children and walk
in the way of love, just as Christ loved us and gave himself up
for us as a fragrant offering and sacrifice to God.*
Ephesians 5:1–2 niv

*B*rad and Emily were captivated by a movie they were watching and didn't notice their toddler, Dakota, make his way over to the front door. He worked very hard trying to figure out how to put on his daddy's work boots. Eventually Brad noticed his son had managed to get his feet into the boots but was unable to stand up. Brad poked Emily and whispered, "Get the camera."

He made his way over to where Dakota was sitting and helped him stand up in the boots. The top of the big boots touched the bottom of Dakota's diaper. The boots were too heavy for Dakota to walk, so he just stood there, smiling. Brad tried hard not to laugh as Emily started snapping pictures.

"He thinks he's doing something really big," Brad said.

"He's trying to be like his daddy," Emily said, smiling. "He is already trying to walk in your shoes!"

Just as children try to imitate their parents, God wants His children to follow His example. His character and nature is expressed throughout the Bible in the lives of those whose story is told there. Follow His example. He will show you His ways.

*Teach me Your ways, Lord, so that I may live
my life following hard after You. Amen.*

This Christmas, God Wants You to Know. . .

He Will Go Before You

"And the LORD, He is the One who goes before you.
He will be with you, He will not leave you nor forsake you;
do not fear nor be dismayed."
DEUTERONOMY 31:8 NKJV

*I*zzy reached out and took her brother Scott's hand. She was very nervous. She had been called as a witness to a crime that took place in her college town. The small community had received national media coverage. She was thankful to have Scott with her since her parents were with her younger sister, who was having a medical procedure done that very day.

"It's okay," Scott said. "Just relax. After this is done, the newspapers will talk about it for a little while longer, and then it will all go away."

"I hope so," she hesitantly replied. Then Scott stopped, and the two sat down on a bench outside the courtroom. "Let's pray," he said. Izzy bowed her head, and Scott prayed. "God, you have promised to go before Izzy. Be with her in the courtroom. Please fill her heart with Your peace and give her the words You want her to say that will penetrate the hearts of the jury so that they may know the truth and do what is right in Your eyes."

Izzy stood up. "I know God is waiting for me inside. I can do this."

God, thank You for going ahead of me and preparing the way.
Give me strength to let go of fear and have faith
that You will see me through. Amen.

This Christmas, God Wants You to Know. . .

EVERYONE'S GOT STUFF

And I know that nothing good lives in me, that is,
in my sinful nature. I want to do what is right, but I can't.
I want to do what is good, but I don't.
I don't want to do what is wrong, but I do it anyway.
ROMANS 7:18–19 NLT

*I*t had been the most difficult Christmas for Jenny. She knew her marriage was over and had been over for a long time. She had gone to counseling, and prayed for God to heal their marriage year after year. Her husband, Tyson, refused to get help, and she couldn't take his emotional and physical abuse anymore. It was affecting the children.

On New Year's Eve, she sat at her dining room table with her friend Emily. She poured her heart out to her. "I feel like such a failure. I've done everything I could do to hold things together. I know God hates divorce."

Emily looked at her and said, "Everyone's got stuff; you can't always see their stuff. We're human, and God knows that. He accepts us as we are. No one sets out to fail. He knows your heart. God can't change us unless we're willing. In marriage—both parties have to be willing."

Thank You for realizing I'm human
and pouring out Your grace on my life.
Help me to remember that everyone's got stuff,
and show me how to extend grace instead of judgment. Amen.

This Christmas, God Wants You to Know...

IT'S OKAY TO BE A CHILD AGAIN

"Truly I tell you, anyone who will not receive the kingdom of God like a little child will never enter it." And he took the children in his arms, placed his hands on them and blessed them.
MARK 10:15–16 NIV

The cousins, Helen, Marsha, and Pam, had become the closest of friends as they grew up, spending most of their summers and holidays at their grandparents' house. As the girls became young women, wives, and mothers, their times together became few and far between. But every few years they made a point to come together—and this year the girls decided to bring all the families together at Helen's parents' house on the lake.

Helen got there first to help her mother in the kitchen. When Marsha and Pam arrived at the same time, they were like little girls again—running, jumping, hugging, and squealing with excitement. They were so thrilled to see one another, Helen's father had to ask them to step back so he and their husbands could have room to bring the luggage through the front door.

The girls stepped back into time, as if they had never been apart, laughing and teasing one another just as they did when they were little. In their hearts for a moment, they were still the same little girls spending special days at Grandma's house.

*Thank You, Father, that I am forever Your child.
Anytime I want, I can climb into Your arms
and be comforted by Your love and grace.*

This Christmas, God Wants You to Know...

HE CREATED YOU FOR HIS PURPOSE

*Then the LORD God formed a man from the dust of the ground
and breathed into his nostrils the breath of life,
and the man became a living being.*

GENESIS 2:7 NIV

Rita found her sixteen-year-old daughter, Myra, in her room, in tears. "Honey, what's wrong?" Myra sniffled and talked through her tears. "I feel so left out. There are Christmas parties, and I've not been invited to one. I can't break into any of the circles—at school or church."

"I know it hurts," Rita said, trying to comfort her daughter. "And the move to a new town during Thanksgiving is a big adjustment. I can't pretend to know what you're going through. I am sorry you're having to go through this."

Myra huffed. "I hate that we had to move and leave all my friends behind. And I thought making new friends would be so much easier than this."

"Praying about it can only help." Myra's face softened, and Rita continued. "I have learned that no one knows the path God has chosen for me better than He does. Spending time with Him reveals the truth and brings about the purpose He designed for us. He knew that purpose before time began, and He has friends for you that have a part in that purpose."

---

*It is amazing to me that before You ever breathed life into the
first man you knew my purpose. Help me to pursue
that purpose with Your grace today. Amen.*

This Christmas, God Wants You to Know. . .

YOUR LIFE IS A PUZZLE HE FITS TOGETHER

*All the days planned for me were written
in your book before I was one day old.*

PSALM 139:16 NCV

Teresa's family rarely used the dining room table, so after their big Christmas dinner, she placed a fresh tablecloth over the table and then poured out a one-thousand-piece puzzle. Then she hid the box with the photo of what the puzzle would eventually look like.

"How are we supposed to do the puzzle without the picture?" her son, Martin, asked.

"Start with edges—put the outside frame together first. Just look for the smooth edges," she told him.

Her daughter, Kimberly, complained, "But Mom! That makes it a lot harder."

Over the next month, the whole family worked off and on to frame the puzzle. One evening Kimberly shouted out, "Mom, I just snapped in the last frame on the puzzle. Now what?"

Teresa called the family together. "Look at this puzzle right now. You were able to frame the picture with what you knew about the frame. Sometimes God only gives you small pieces of the puzzle of your life. You don't know what the big picture looks like, but you trust that if you follow the pieces He's given you, then it will all fit together in the end, and you'll see the big picture."

*Help me to be patient as I discover how the pieces
of my life fit together in Your perfect plan. Amen.*

This Christmas, God Wants You to Know. . .

THERE ARE NO REAL SHORTCUTS DURING CONSTRUCTION

*Therefore judge nothing before the appointed time;
wait until the LORD comes. He will bring to light what
is hidden in darkness and will expose the motives of the heart.*
1 CORINTHIANS 4:5 NIV

*I*f you live in the city, most likely there is road construction going on somewhere all the time. It's usually a mess—especially in the winter, with mud, potholes, and delays caused by the slowdown to one lane. You crawl through it every day, take a detour to avoid it, or look for a shortcut if it's along your daily commute.

UNDER CONSTRUCTION signs signal the road is in a temporary state of transition—a work in progress. It's not finished yet. There is still an anticipation that when it's done, you'll have a wonderful, fresh, and new road to navigate. Right now, though, you have to slow down, maneuver around men working and equipment, and even take detours sometimes.

Sometimes that's what it's like for us as believers. God has a destiny and a purpose. Perhaps you've thought, *I sure wish He'd hurry.* God is committed to the process of building your destiny. He doesn't take any shortcuts. He's the master builder, and you can trust Him to complete the work in His precise time.

*Forgive me, Lord, for my impatience as I trust You on my
journey. I don't want to take the shortcuts; I'd rather
travel the path You have for me. Amen.*

This Christmas, God Wants You to Know. . .

HE IS ALWAYS WITH YOU

"Behold, the virgin shall conceive and bear a son,
and they shall call his name Immanuel" (which means, God with us).
MATTHEW 1:23 ESV

Nicholas, only five, was mesmerized by the Christmas decorations. He went with his father out to the garage and watched as he carried in the tree and several big boxes. He ran his fingers over the beautiful tree ornaments, careful to touch them gently. "Look at this," his mother called. "It's a Nativity scene."

"Ooohh!" Nicholas exclaimed as he caught a glimpse of baby Jesus in the picture on the box. "Let me hold baby Jesus, please, please," he said, bouncing up and down with his hands outstretched.

Nicholas spent many an evening mesmerized by baby Jesus on the coffee table in the living room. His mother explained this wasn't the real Jesus that was all grown up in his heart, along with several other teaching opportunities as they presented themselves throughout the Christmas celebration. When it came time to box up the Christmas decorations and send them back to the garage, Nicholas said, "You can't put baby Jesus in the garage."

Unsure of how to respond, his mother offered, "Where should we put him?" Nicholas excitedly bounced up and down and replied, "Let him stay in my room."

May I never bring out Christmas like I bring out
a box of decorations. Let the real celebration
always be alive in my heart! Amen.

This Christmas, God Wants You to Know. . .

We All Need More Singing

"Whoever offers praise glorifies Me; and to him who orders his conduct aright I will show the salvation of God."
Psalm 50:23 nkjv

*A*nnie worked in a stressful environment as the office manager in a large insurance office downtown. It took all she had to stay positive, especially during the holidays, and she used music to keep her heart light. She had a tune on her lips almost all the time. It served as a barrier to the negative complaints from her staff and coworkers.

Most enjoyed her positive outlook. One team member commented, "I can always expect to see sunshine coming from your soul, no matter what's going on around here." But unexpectedly, one afternoon her boss scolded her for singing. "Why are you always singing? This is a professional environment, and that's not professional."

Annie smiled in spite of the scowl on his face. "Respectfully, sir," she said, "I guess I could be just like everyone else here. I could complain and gripe about every little thing I don't like. But instead, a song in my heart and on my lips keeps me upbeat, lighthearted, and able to handle almost anything that comes my way—including the bad attitudes and unprofessionalism I experience from your team on a daily basis."

He cracked a half smile and nodded. "Carry on, then," he said.

Lord, let the light of Your presence shine out from me as I give You praise each day. Amen.

This Christmas, God Wants You to Know. . .

YOU HAVE AN INVISIBLE COUNSELOR

The Spirit of the LORD shall rest upon him, the Spirit of wisdom
and understanding, the Spirit of counsel and might,
the Spirit of knowledge and the fear of the LORD.
ISAIAH 11:2 ESV

*E*ach person has an individual journey. The Bible is a guideline for the ways God desires for you to live your life, but it doesn't tell you specific answers to some of the everyday choices and decisions you have to make along the way. Life can be unclear and may not make sense at times. That is why He sent you an invisible Counselor.

In those times you don't know the direction to go, the choice to make, or maybe even how to pray, the Holy Spirit will speak to your heart with wisdom in the midst of circumstances and assist you as you navigate life.

As you listen for His counsel, the answers will come. He can give you strategies and ideas. He's a gentleman and must be invited in. He will not press Himself on you. When you welcome Him, He'll give you the answers you need. He'll show you what career is right for you, what job to take, where to live, whom to date or marry, and how to raise your children.

When you find yourself stuck in a hard place, He will whisper direction. As you act on His instruction, you can see the whole thing turn around.

Holy Spirit, I invite You to be my invisible Counselor—
let's do life together. Amen.

This Christmas, God Wants You to Know. . .

WORDS OF THANKS SPEAK TO THE HEART

But you are a chosen race, a royal priesthood, a holy nation,
a people for his own possession, that you may proclaim the excellencies
of him who called you out of darkness into his marvelous light.
1 PETER 2:9 ESV

One of the greatest losses ever experienced is when you don't take the opportunity to tell people why you are thankful for them. A verbal acknowledgment for the things and people we are thankful for speaks to the heart of God and the people in your life.

Have you ever been to a funeral where they say wonderful things about the person who has died and regret never telling him or her those things? People are dying for affirmation. Your husband would love for you to say, "Thanks for being such a great provider for our family." Your wife would like to hear you say, "I appreciate how you express such love and tenderness to our children." Your friends would enjoy hearing you express how their listening ear or positive encouragement helped you get through a difficult time.

Feeling grateful and not expressing it is like wrapping a gift and never giving it. Don't wait until they're gone to realize you have unwrapped gifts you still want to give. Cultivate thanksgiving in your heart, and express it to others.

Now is the time to express your thanks. Write the note! Express the love!

Lord, I want to live my life "thank-filled" so I always have
a natural tendency to overflow with thanks! Amen.

This Christmas, God Wants You to Know. . .

JESUS COUNTED THE COST

He is so rich in kindness and grace that he purchased our freedom
with the blood of his Son and forgave our sins.
EPHESIANS 1:7 NLT

Every choice, every decision comes at a price. Whether you take action or refuse to take action—there is a cost associated. It may or may not be financial in nature. It could cost you emotionally, physically, spiritually, or relationally. The decision to drive faster than the speed limit could cost you a speeding ticket, a car accident, or no consequences at all. What you choose to put into your body often determines how healthy you are or aren't.

Jesus counted the cost to come to the earth as a baby on that first Christmas Day. He willingly left His place in heaven to live in a body that would ultimately experience a painful death. He submitted to the will of the heavenly Father by laying down His life. He gave a life that was only His to give so that everyone could experience an eternal life with Him.

It was the highest price that could have been paid—and yet He endured it all for a relationship with you, God's ultimate creation. You are valuable and considered a pearl of great price. What does your relationship with God cost you? What are you willing to pay to know Him more?

Thank You for Your willingness to give Your life for mine.
Help me to live my life pleasing to You. Amen.

This Christmas, God Wants You to Know. . .

THERE IS POWER IN UNITY

*Behold, how good and how pleasant it is for
brethren to dwell together in unity!*
PSALM 133:1 NKJV

Since the twins were born, Stephen and Esther weren't communicating, and when they did, it usually ended up in a fight. Stephen shared his frustrations with Bill, an older family friend. "I'm really struggling, and I don't know what to do. We fight a lot. When I get home, the house is a mess; sometimes dinner isn't ready; and it looks like Esther did nothing all day long."

Bill smiled. "Esther probably feels unappreciated because you don't see all the work that goes on throughout the day. You should take two hours and let her go out—then see how much you get done with two little ones to watch."

Stephen frowned. "I guess you're right."

Then Bill looked at him intently. "If you don't do something—your marriage could become a casualty. Your relationship has a new dynamic. Do you realize that you set the atmosphere of your home with your words?"

"My words haven't been positive lately," Stephen confessed. "I've complained lately about the house being a mess, and I even asked her, 'What did you do all day?'"

Bill continued, "Refuse to let the little annoyances destroy your relationship. Focus on harmony, and set a positive tone in your home and with Esther. You will see a change right away."

*Lord, put a guard over my lips so that I may speak words
that bring harmony and peace. Amen.*

This Christmas, God Wants You to Know. . .

YOUR THOUGHTS DETERMINE YOUR ATTITUDE

For as [a man] thinks in his heart, so is he.
PROVERBS 23:7 NKJV

*B*arbie and Kristin had always been friends, but after a difficult divorce and a struggle for Kristin to get back into the workplace, Barbie's encouragement and support did nothing to sweeten Kristin's sour attitude.

She began to avoid Kristin's phone calls and text messages. It had been weeks since they'd met for coffee or lunch. Barbie had some issues of her own with her older son and his sudden lack of attention to his schoolwork, and her grandfather was very ill. She didn't think she could handle Kristin's negative noise, too!

One afternoon Kristin dropped by Barbie's office and stuck her head into her office. "Hey!" she said. "Are you avoiding me?"

Barbie replied, "Forgive me, but yes, I am." Kristin looked sad, and Barbie said, "I love you, but I have stuff going on in my own life, and I just don't have the strength to deal with your negativity. You hardly ever say anything positive about yourself anymore."

Kristin was hurt at first and left abruptly. As she thought about her good friend's words, she realized she was right. She texted Barbie later and thanked her for her honesty.

Your attitude is a projection of your thoughts. If you need an attitude adjustment, compare what you're thinking to the instruction from God's Word.

Lord, help me tell myself Your truth.
I choose to align my thoughts to Your Word each day. Amen.

This Christmas, God Wants You to Know. . .

THERE IS A CHURCH HOME FOR YOU

As each has received a gift, use it to serve one another,
as good stewards of God's varied grace.
1 PETER 4:10 ESV

Kayla knocked on her new roommate Samantha's door. She took her loud moan as approval to enter. She opened the door to find her still in bed. "Hey! Aren't you going to church?"

Samantha slowly stuck her head out of the covers. "Oh, man! I really wasn't planning on it. Since moving here, I've just not connected to any of the churches I've visited."

"Yeah, I know. It was hard for me at first, too," Kayla replied. "But you've got to keep looking until you know where you fit. It's important to be around others who can support you, encourage you, and pray with you."

"You do all those things for me, roomie," Samantha teased.

"It's really important to me that you find a church and get involved. I really messed up when I first moved here. Like you, it was my first time on my own. I got in with the wrong crowd and started partying, sleeping in, and skipping church. None of us are immune to temptation. I just don't want to see you go through that."

Samantha smiled at Kayla. "Thank you for caring enough to challenge me to be accountable to God. I'll get ready and go to your church with you today."

Please place the right people in my life that
will help me stay accountable to You. Amen.

This Christmas, God Wants You to Know. . .

It's Important to Safeguard Your Heart

Guard your heart above all else,
for it determines the course of your life.
PROVERBS 4:23 NLT

Coleen and Blake decided to buy an older home, built in the fifties, with lots of character. Coleen was a little nervous but asked if their friends Kate and Phil, who had come into town for the weekend, would like to see the house. They said they would. As they gave them the grand tour, Kate and Phil both pointed out the great architecture from that era and how the old tiles in the bathrooms were so authentic, and they went on and on about the beautiful hardwood floors that had never been stained that lay under the carpet.

When they got back in the car, Coleen took a deep breath and excitedly exclaimed, "I am so thrilled you liked the house. You saw all the potential we could see in it and completely affirmed our dream of what this house could be."

Kate asked, "Why wouldn't we? It's amazing!"

Blake piped up from the driver's seat, "We showed it to another couple, and they stomped on our dream. They couldn't get past how much work it was going to be and how they would never buy an older home."

Phil smiled. "Yes, you have to guard your heart when it comes to sharing your dreams. Thank you for trusting us with yours."

God, teach me to guard my heart above all else
because it determines the course of my life. Amen.

This Christmas, God Wants You to Know. . .

TEARS ARE A LANGUAGE HE UNDERSTANDS

When Jesus saw Mary crying and the Jews who came with her also
crying, he was upset and was deeply troubled. He asked,
"Where did you bury him?" "Come and see, Lord," they said. Jesus cried.
So the Jews said, "See how much he loved him."
JOHN 11:33–36 NCV

*P*erhaps there have been times in your life where you thought the tears would never end. Maybe you spent many nights wondering where God was and why He had not intervened in your situation.

Jesus wasn't in town when His friend Lazarus died. They sent word to Him that Lazarus was near death, but Jesus didn't go to him immediately. Days passed before He made His way to them. Surely Mary wondered what was more important than coming and healing Lazarus.

He greeted Mary and a group of others, and they were in tears, grieving the loss of a brother and friend. And then Jesus wept, too. People remarked about how much He must have loved Lazarus because of the grief accompanied by weeping they saw from Him. He came to the tomb of a loved one He cared for deeply.

If tears have ever been your companion for weeks at a time, God knows your story. When there are no words to express the emotions inside, tears fall and communicate a heartbreak that could never be uttered with words.

Lord, thank You for understanding my tears
when I have no words. Amen.

This Christmas, God Wants You to Know. . .

HE CARES FOR THE LOST

"I will search for the lost and bring back the strays.
I will bind up the injured and strengthen the weak, but the sleek
and the strong I will destroy. I will shepherd the flock with justice."
EZEKIEL 34:16 NIV

Donna went out into the backyard to check on Rosey, her two-year-old German Shepherd. The snow was coming down hard. As she picked up the water bowl and set it inside to thaw, she panicked at the sight of the back gate ajar. *How could it have come opened?* she wondered.

She called for Rosey, but she didn't come to her. She was gone. She hoped she hadn't lost her tags on her collar. She ran down the alley and around to the street. The neighbors all knew her dog. She asked the boys sliding down the street on a trash can lid if they'd seen her. They all shook their heads no. She asked Mr. Martin about her at the mailbox as well as Mrs. Sims, who was cleaning the snow off her front porch.

Donna went back into the house and asked the Lord to bring her safely home. About an hour later, she bundled up to go out again. As she reached to open the door, a man stood there with Rosey. "I think this is your dog. . . ," he started as Rosey bounced into Donna's arms.

***

God, You care about all lost things.
Thank You for finding me and bringing me
safely into Your loving arms. Amen.

This Christmas, God Wants You to Know. . .

YOU ARE A WITNESS

You have left your old sinful life and the things you did before.
You have begun to live the new life, in which you are being
made new and are becoming like the One who made you.
This new life brings you the true knowledge of God.
COLOSSIANS 3:9–10 NCV

A group of older guys met each weekday morning at the local doughnut shop in a little town to chitchat and trade stories about their day. This particular group of guys had been meeting for years, but the group noticed a change in their buddy Ray.

While Ray was getting his coffee and doughnuts, he became the topic of conversation at his own table. "Oh, he's still funny and has the same charismatic personality," Phil told Clay. "But something's different. I just can't put my finger on it."

"He doesn't seem as angry," Clay replied. "And have you noticed, he doesn't tell off-color jokes anymore. I haven't really heard him curse much."

"Yeah," Frank chimed in. "He doesn't laugh at those jokes, either, just kinda gets quiet and looks down."

"You guys know I can hear you," Ray said, setting his coffee down on the table.

The men chuckled. "So what gives?" Fred asked. "Are you going to tell us you got religion or something?"

"I have a new relationship with God. I like the new person I'm becoming. I'm not perfect, but I'm definitely different."

I want to be an example of Your great mercy and love.
Let others see You in me. Amen.

This Christmas, God Wants You to Know. . .

YOU'RE GOING TO MAKE IT

Jesus said, "Don't let your hearts be troubled. Trust in God,
and trust in me. There are many rooms in my Father's house;
I would not tell you this if it were not true. I am going there to
prepare a place for you. After I go and prepare a place for you, I will
come back and take you to be with me so that you may be where I am."
JOHN 14:1–3 NCV

*C*ammie worked full-time and had teenagers at home. She seldom did anything for herself. Her time and energy were given to adding to the family income or pouring into her husband and children. Still, she wasn't confident she was doing things right. She felt her parenting skills were less than adequate. She constantly second-guessed her parenting decisions.

When they moved to a new town for her husband's job, they began attending a small church close to their new home. There God connected her with a friend and mentor unlike anyone she'd ever met.

This woman, Leanna, oozed with the love of God. "She dripped with encouragement but not the fakey kind I can't stand," she told her husband. "She's genuine." As their friendship grew, Cammie opened her heart and allowed Leanna to speak positive affirmations into her life. Years after her children were out on their own, she could hear Leanna's words to her: "Baby, you're going to make it!"

Thank You for the people You bring into my life
to speak the truth and encourage me. Amen.

This Christmas, God Wants You to Know. . .

He Cares When Your Heart Is Hurting

"The Lord has put his Spirit in me, because he appointed me to tell the Good News to the poor. He has sent me to tell the captives they are free and to tell the blind that they can see again."

Luke 4:18 ncv

The emotional pain of Josie's broken heart went unnoticed by most this first Christmas without her mother. Her heartbreak left no broken bones, bruises, or visible scars, but the pain was real and deep. Her mother died unexpectedly, and now, months later, the emotional pain Josie had buried began to ooze out. She experienced agonizing pain in her neck, back, and shoulders. She went to her doctor, and his first question was, "Have you experienced any major stress or loss in your life recently?"

Shocked that he had touched a wound that she'd tried to keep hidden from everyone, she said, "Yes!" and told him about her mother. The doctor was able to treat her physical symptoms, but he had no way to help with her broken heart.

Josie decided it was time to acknowledge her grief and let God in. She had been afraid that if she opened her heart a little, then everything she'd been trying to hold in would erupt like a volcano and she would not be able to regain her composure. Now she was ready to let go and let God begin to heal and restore her emotionally.

I trust my emotions to You today.
Restore me completely in every area of my life. Amen.

This Christmas, God Wants You to Know. . .

WHEN YOU LOOK FOR HIM, YOU WILL FIND HIM

Then you will call upon Me and go and pray to Me,
and I will listen to you. And you will seek Me and find Me,
when you search for Me with all your heart.
JEREMIAH 29:12–13 NKJV

Shara located several flashlights for the kids to take with them to a Christmas party lock-in. "Have you ever played hide and seek at night, Mom?" her fourteen-year-old, Matthew, asked.

"Oh, yes," she replied with enthusiasm. "There's nothing like playing hide and seek with your friends late at night; it's frightening and exciting at the same time."

"Sometimes," Matthew confessed, "I let them find me because of the thrill of connecting. The girls squeal and giggle and give their location away, so they are easy to find."

"Well, have a great time," she called as she heard the honk of their friend's van, "and don't forget your coats. It's going to be cold out there in the snow."

The house was suddenly quiet, and Shara thought about her son's words, "Sometimes I let them find me." She thought about the last few days and the chaos going on in her life. Christmas always brought busyness. She realized she hadn't really spent time with the Lord. She imagined that maybe her time with Him was like hide and seek in the dark. As she got quiet she imagined Him allowing her to seek and find Him.

Lord, I lay aside the worries of my heart
and make You a priority right now. Amen.

This Christmas, God Wants You to Know. . .

GUILT AND SHAME NO LONGER BELONG TO YOU

Christ had no sin, but God made him become sin so that
in Christ we could become right with God.
2 CORINTHIANS 5:21 NCV

D. L. Moody said, "God has cast our confessed sins into the depths of the sea, and He's even put a 'No Fishing' sign over the spot." Guilt can eat at you, if you let it. When you think about the consequences of your sin after you have asked for forgiveness, it will only do harm to your heart. "What if" and "if only" are both entrances to a journey down memory lane that ends in devastation.

Jesus, who knew no sin, became sin for you. He died a criminal's death although He was innocent and went to hell for no other reason than to pay the price for every sin ever committed.

While it's good to learn from your mistakes, God doesn't want you to torture yourself over them. It doesn't benefit you to replay your mistakes over and over in your mind. He forgives and forgets and expects you to do the same.

God desires relationship because of that amazing love He has for you. Jesus paid that price, was raised from the dead, and was triumphant over Satan so you could be restored and given the opportunity to come blameless into God's presence. When you understand this truth, you can live your life free of guilt and shame.

Lord, thank You for giving me freedom from guilt and shame.
Help me to let it go. Amen.

This Christmas, God Wants You to Know. . .

HE WANTS TO BE FIRST PLACE

Do nothing out of selfish ambition or vain conceit. Rather,
in humility value others above yourselves, not looking to your own
interests but each of you to the interests of the others.
PHILIPPIANS 2:3–4 NIV

The Christmas season was always full, but this year Ally had a new job with a heavy training schedule and was also newly engaged. With work, a June wedding date, and the normal Christmas busyness, she found herself completely out of patience most days.

Her best friend, Christine, sat next to her on the couch, turning the pages of the December bridal magazines. She wasted little time broaching the subject of Ally's crummy attitude gently. "I've noticed you're not your normal self. What's up?"

"Honestly?" Ally huffed. Then her eyes filled with tears, and her voice softened. "I'm not spending time with the Lord. I haven't spent time studying His Word since Jason proposed. I've made no time for my daily exchange with Him. . .and I am so ashamed to admit it."

"Good!" Christine said, smiling. "You told the truth. And you know God wants to be first place. It's His love flowing in you and through you that allow you to be the person everyone loves."

Ally smiled. "You're so right. Will you pray with me about this now?" Christine nodded and bowed her head.

Lord, remind me spend time with You first—
no matter how busy I am. Amen.

This Christmas, God Wants You to Know. . .

It's Worth the Wait

Wait on the LORD; be of good courage,
and He shall strengthen your heart; wait, I say, on the LORD!
PSALM 27:14 NKJV

*H*ave you ever had a child find where you had hidden the Christmas presents before Christmas Day—spoiling the surprise on Christmas morning? Maybe you were that child.

The thrill and excitement of opening something unknown and special is gone. Each gift is already known. Not only are these children disappointed, but they also feel guilty for not waiting or fearful of being found out when their lack of excitement gives them away. The parents are disappointed because they missed experiencing the joy and elation the gift giving brings to them in seeing the surprise and joy on their child's face.

Getting ahead of God and trying to make something happen on your own can be similar to opening all your presents before Christmas Day. Perhaps the joy is lost because you feel like you've disobeyed your Father.

Doing things God's way brings pleasure to Him because you open the gifts in your life in the order and timing He has for them. When you're tempted to hurry things along by doing things your way, remember His ways are perfect. Trust Him to bring His perfect gifts to you in His time and season so you can enjoy them and bring Him pleasure.

Father, no matter how bad I want to experience all You've
promised, give me grace and patience to wait on You. Amen.

This Christmas, God Wants You to Know. . .

JESUS IS YOUR DOORWAY TO THE SPIRIT-LED LIFE

Since we are living by the Spirit,
let us follow the Spirit's leading in every part of our lives.
GALATIANS 5:25 NLT

*A*udrey looked down at the pile of clothes she'd stacked next to the washing machine. She began the weekly task of turning her boys' jeans, socks, and shirts right-side out before dropping them into the washing machine. It seemed nearly impossible for them to shed a thread of clothing without them turning inside out.

Suddenly she had an interesting thought and called her mom, Janice, who had dropped in for coffee, to come to the laundry room. "Mom," she said, "this is what it must have looked like to God when Adam and Eve sinned—everything that was once on the inside came out, and what was on the outside turned in."

"Yes," Janice agreed. "Adam could see, hear, taste, touch, and smell from both a physical and spiritual standpoint. I believe he saw God with his spiritual eyes and heard Him with spiritual ears. Sin severed their connection. Where their spiritual senses had been dominant, their physical senses became their main means to gather information and learn about their new world outside the garden, where they once walked with God."

"That is why we need Jesus," Audrey continued. "He is the doorway to return us to a Spirit-led life. He can take us from living wrong-side out to right-side out."

Jesus, thank You for opening the door for me
to live the Spirit-led life. Amen.

This Christmas, God Wants You to Know. . .

WHEN YOU STEP NEAR TO GOD, HE STEPS NEAR TO YOU

Draw near to God, and he will draw near to you. Cleanse your hands, you sinners, and purify your hearts, you double-minded.
JAMES 4:8 ESV

Grace was on her own. She had always dreamed of moving to the big city and making her mark on the fashion industry. Two months into her dream, it wasn't going so well. She had big plans but found herself working in a coffee shop to make ends meet.

Now bills were coming due; money was really tight. She wasn't sure she was going to make it this month. Christmas was coming, and she would not be able to fly home to see family. She called her mom. "I just don't understand why the doors aren't opening. I wanted this to work. I've done everything to make it work."

Her mother tried to comfort her. "Honey, have you connected with a local church? You need to feed your spirit. You need the support and encouragement of other believers. God works through relationships. Are you doing it your way or giving God room to do things His way?"

Her mother's words stung, but she knew it was the truth. After she got off the phone, she spent some time in prayer. Suddenly, it was as if God Himself wrapped His arms around her. She was determined this time to do things His way!

Thank You for being there every time I reach out to You. Amen.

64

This Christmas, God Wants You to Know. . .

HE BUILDS YOUR LIFE WITH FAITH

Love and faithfulness meet together;
righteousness and peace kiss each other.
PSALM 85:10 NIV

Susan and Wayne had not intended to build a house in their retirement years, but after traveling for several years in their motor home, they felt it was time to settle down. They had really enjoyed a home they had rented on the lake at one time, but there were no homes that met their criteria.

So they bought a plot of land that was set off from the lake, close to the rental home they were moving out of. They found a builder and drew up house plans. They watched as the foundation was poured, the plumbing went in, and the walls went up. They could only imagine what it would look and feel like. After six months of hard work, excitement, frustration, and a few tears, and they were able to move into their new home.

One evening a few days before Christmas, they sat together on their back porch watching the sun set over the cold, blue lake. "As I watched this house go up," Wayne said, "it reminded me of how God builds our lives. His Word, much like the blueprint for the house, gives direction to the frame, but then faith adds all the little extra things that finish it out."

Susan smiled. "We have certainly watched the pieces of our lives come together over the years, specifically by His design."

When I doubt Your plans, remind me to trust You
to build my life according to Your perfect designs. Amen.

This Christmas, God Wants You to Know. . .

YOU CONTROL WHAT YOU THINK ABOUT

For "who has known the mind of the LORD that he may
instruct Him?" But we have the mind of Christ.
1 CORINTHIANS 2:16 NKJV

*D*o you ever feel like your thoughts are carrying on a conversation in your head?" Mariah asked her friend Casey. "Sometimes it feels like the things I am concerned about take flight and I can't get off the plane."

Casey looked around the coffee shop and then back to her friend. "Your thoughts are your choice. You control what you think about. I used to worry about everything. I would run scenarios in my mind of the different what-ifs. It made me crazy."

"So, what did you do?" Mariah asked, leaning into Casey across the table.

"I practiced a new habit until it became a permanent behavior. When a negative thought comes, I counter it with a positive thought or action—like how much God must love me. I remind myself of Bible promises. I remember the times when God has brought me through a hard time."

"That's so freeing," Mariah said, sighing. "I want to do that. I want to change my thoughts so I can truly live by faith. When I start sharing negative thoughts with you, will you help me remember to change my thoughts and my words?"

"More than happy to," Casey said with a smile.

Lord, when I get lost in negative thinking, please help me to change my thoughts. Remind me of Your faithfulness. Amen.

This Christmas, God Wants You to Know. . .

HE WANTS ALL OF YOU

My son, give me your heart and let your eyes delight in my ways.
PROVERBS 23:26 NIV

There is no better place to live than in that place of surrender to the One who loves you most and knows you best. He knows about the secrets of your heart—those things you are reluctant to give completely to Him. Perhaps it's a habit you hold on to or a hurt you refuse to forgive. Maybe it's a dream you really want that you think He may not have in His plans for you.

The universal sign of surrender is upraised hands. As a small child you lifted your hands in surrender, wanting those you love to take you in their arms and care for you. Your heavenly Father desires for you to come to Him like a child. You may not understand everything He is doing, but you trust Him completely, allowing Him to lead, guide, and direct you.

When you come before God in prayer, relinquish everything: offer your body as a living sacrifice upon His altar. Give your soul and all you desire willingly to Him. He wants all of you given freely without reservation. He has promised to give you an abundant life—a life that is more than you could ask or even think.

Today, I give You all of me. I hold nothing back.
Take my life, transform me, and use me for Your glory.
Amen.

This Christmas, God Wants You to Know. . .

It's Not about Your Performance

*For it is by grace you have been saved,
through faith—and this is not from yourselves,
it is the gift of God—not by works, so that no one can boast.*
Ephesians 2:8–9 niv

Joy sat on the front row waiting for the preschool Christmas program to start. It was the first time her son, Caden, was old enough to perform. As the children filed in and took their seats, Caden's two-year-old class went straight to the platform, no doubt to let them go first since keeping their attention for long was out of the question. Joy was thrilled to see her son there. He saw her and waved, wiggled, squirmed, and made faces while the other children sang songs. One little girl nearly fell down competing with classmates to stand in front of the microphone.

Suddenly, Caden was distracted. He had noticed the clear, acrylic podium off to the side of the stage. He completely disengaged from the performance and made his way straight to the podium. He stood under the top of it and pressed his hands and face to it like he would a car window. He "smooshed" his nose and licked the podium. He was giving a performance of his own.

Joy thought, *I am so grateful that God isn't worried about my performance. It's His grace that makes me His.*

---

*Thank You, Lord, for giving me Your grace.
It's nothing I've done and everything You've done
that provides me each day with hope. Amen.*

This Christmas, God Wants You to Know. . .

HE MAKES YOU BRAND NEW

And the one sitting on the throne said, "Look, I am making
everything new!" And then he said to me, "Write this down,
for what I tell you is trustworthy and true."
REVELATION 21:5 NLT

*E*ach year Grammy purchased new clothes for her grandchildren to wear to the Christmas Eve celebration at their church. Four-year-old Emma pressed her dress down as she sat on the bench in the foyer in front of the Christmas tree. "Grammy," she began, "why do you buy me a pretty dress with matching bows, frilly socks, and new shoes for Christmas church? Is it so I can look more pretty, 'cause it's Christmas and all?"

Grammy sat down next to Emma. "Well, it's nice to have new clothes and look pretty, but this is a family tradition." Emma looked puzzled.

"I buy new clothes for Christmas to remind me that Jesus was born so that every person could have a new, clean start with God. Just like you put on your new clothes and dress pretty, God gives you His best every day."

"So, I get a new dress because Jesus was born to make me a new person?"

"Yes!" Grammy said. "You have been made new because Jesus came into your heart. He made your heart clean and helps you make good choices." Emma smiled.

Thank You that I don't have to stay the same
but have been made new in You, Father. Amen.

This Christmas, God Wants You to Know. . .

There Is Strength in Godly Relationships

And let us not neglect our meeting together,
as some people do, but encourage one another,
especially now that the day of his return is drawing near.
Hebrews 10:25 nlt

I don't know what the big deal is about going to church," Erica commented to her husband, Rob. "We work so hard throughout the week and have all kinds of activities going on with the kids. It's just difficult to get up and go to church."

"I'm guessing you got a phone call from your sister about the Christmas services," Rob commented.

"No, my mother, this time," she replied.

Their nine-year-old son, Marcus, rounded the corner into the kitchen and said, "I like church. When I get to go, I am happier and nicer to my friends."

Rob looked at Erica. "Out of the mouth of babes. . . ," he said, his voice trailing off as Marcus left the kitchen.

"He's right about that," Erica said softly. "I am more positive and stronger in my faith when I go to church, hear God's Word taught, and connect to strong believers who will encourage me."

"Sometimes when I'm discouraged, I'll get an e-mail from one of the men's group leaders. They help me stay accountable to God, myself, and my family," Rob admitted. "I think it's time we make a commitment to be in church every Sunday. Are you in?" Erica nodded in agreement.

Lord, help me keep my commitment to stay
connected to my church family. Amen.

This Christmas, God Wants You to Know. . .

IT'S NEVER TOO LATE FOR A MIRACLE

"And whatever you ask in My name, that I will do,
that the Father may be glorified in the Son.
If you ask anything in My name, I will do it."
JOHN 14:13–14 NKJV

Olivia's father disappeared from her life for the most part when she was twelve years old. There were no birthday cards, Christmas presents, phone calls, or daddy-daughter dates. He was in another state, living in his own world. He was an alcoholic, and the physical and emotional abuse toward her mother extinguished him from her life. It was his choice. He could have stayed connected, but he seemed—to Olivia—to have moved on. He remarried and started a new family.

In high school, sometimes Olivia imagined he would just appear. She prayed he would change through the miraculous power of God. Olivia's mother was a Christian and had raised her all her life in church. She prayed and asked God to save her father and restore her relationship with him.

After Olivia had a family of her own, she initiated contact with her father, only to be disappointed. Still, Olivia continued to pray for a miracle in her father's life. God answered her prayer at her oldest son's high school graduation. Her father showed up clean and sober for six months because of his new relationship with God.

You are a miracle maker.
Thank You that it's never too late for a miracle in my life.
Help me to believe no matter how long it takes. Amen.

This Christmas, God Wants You to Know. . .

His Grace Will Help You Walk It Out

For the grace of God has appeared that offers salvation to all people.
It teaches us to say "No" to ungodliness and worldly passions,
and to live self-controlled, upright and godly lives in this present age.
TITUS 2:11–12 NIV

*D*avid was the son his father forgot and the instrument God desired to use to lead His people—the nation of Israel. His father, Jesse, left him outside with the sheep when the prophet Samuel asked to see his sons. His own father rejected him as one God might choose as king. When the prophet Samuel found him, he was still a teenager, but God gave him a promise that he would become king of Israel.

There were many great victories and terrible failures before the promise was ever realized. Still a teen, he slayed a lion and a bear to protect his father's sheep and took down the giant, Goliath, with a single stone and sling. He found favor with the king, who later became jealous and pursued him in order to kill him. He slept with another man's wife and murdered him to cover his sin. Yet, he was quick to repent, and his heart was tender toward God.

David's journey reveals that forgiveness from God does not mean you can escape the consequences of sinful actions, but it offers His grace to walk it out.

Heavenly Father, thank You for Your assurance that
no matter what circumstances I face, You have
given me Your grace to walk it out. Amen.

This Christmas, God Wants You to Know. . .

IT MATTERS WHAT YOU SAY

Death and life are in the power of the tongue,
and those who love it will eat its fruit.
PROVERBS 18:21 NKJV

Driving through the icy streets, Daniel swerved to give a couple walking on the street more space. When he did, a frozen tree branch in the road was caught under his tire and flipped upward, slapping the backside of his driver-side mirror. "Oh! Great!" he exclaimed to himself. "More money out the window. . .at least another hundred dollars to get that fixed." He had a crummy attitude this Christmas. He wanted to go home to the warmer Arizona climate, but his parents had made plans to go out of town the day after Christmas.

Later that evening, while FaceTiming his girlfriend, Shelley, he lamented to her about all the disappointments December had brought his way. "At least we'll be together on Christmas Day," she said. "You know, the devil wants to steal all that Christmas represents. He wants to silence the celebration, and you're helping him by grumbling and complaining about every little challenge that comes your way."

"You're right," Daniel admitted. "I've thought if things were different, I would feel like celebrating. Thanks, Shelley. I needed to hear the truth. I am changing my words today from complaint to celebration."

Thank You, God, that Christmas has nothing to do with me and everything to do with what You did through Jesus for me. Amen.

This Christmas, God Wants You to Know. . .

IT'S BETTER TO PLEASE GOD THAN MEN

*Obviously, I'm not trying to win the approval of people, but of God.
If pleasing people were my goal, I would not be Christ's servant.*
GALATIANS 1:10 NLT

Savannah, Callie's oldest daughter, was born a pleaser.
When she was tempted to disobey as a toddler, all Callie had
to do was give her a look of disapproval, and she complied.
She hardly ever had to discipline her. She wanted the
approval and applause of her parents—at least until now.

Then Callie noticed a change. The defiance grew worse
with the Christmas break from school. Her alliance seemed
to shift from her parents to her peers. The once-agreeable
child suddenly resisted everything. Discipline became hard,
and their relationship became strained. Communication
was difficult because it seemed Savannah challenged her on
everything. Callie began to ask God what she needed to do
differently.

She asked God to open Savannah's heart to the things
God gave her to say to her. She began to gently talk to her
about looking for God's approval in the choices and decisions she made instead of the approval of her friends. She
shared how she had failed in her own life in that area and
it became common ground for mother-daughter conversa-
tions. It was a beginning, and Callie was thankful.

*Give me the courage to seek Your approval above anyone else's.
Amen.*

This Christmas, God Wants You to Know. . .

ALL YOU HAVE TO DO IS FOLLOW

This is what you were called to do, because Christ suffered for you
and gave you an example to follow. So you should do as he did.
1 PETER 2:21 NCV

*P*eter and Charlotte had moved their family across the United States several times for Peter's career. Each time the travel from the old city to the new one got easier for Charlotte, but the very first move was a nightmare.

The kids were really little then. Peter had taken the older two with him in the U-Haul, and Charlotte followed him with their toddler in the car with her. Between Albuquerque and Amarillo, Charlotte had slowed down and eventually lost sight of Peter and the U-Haul. She sped up, thinking she would eventually find him. They didn't have cell phones back then. She pulled over and waited then circled back, waiting for him. Hours later he found her, but that moment was always referred to as a low point in their marriage.

Now Charlotte was a professional follower. She stayed with Peter, no matter what. If he went through a yellow light, she went, too. If he stopped for gas, she stopped, too. She joked with her friends that she had become a professional follower. She could follow anyone, anywhere—and they couldn't lose her—even if they tried.

Lord, help me to become a professional follower. No matter
where You go, I want to follow hard after You. Amen.

This Christmas, God Wants You to Know. . .

HE WILL FINISH WHAT HE STARTED

The LORD will perfect that which concerns me; Your mercy,
O LORD, endures forever; do not forsake the works of Your hands.
PSALM 138:8 NKJV

*A*mber had really struggled with what she wanted to be when she grew up. Her parents had called her their "forever student" as she tried different areas of study. She had finally achieved her bachelor's degree after seven years of school—with jobs and different adventures in between.

She wanted to pursue a graduate degree, but school loans pressed her to get a full-time job. So she set her goals the last semester of school and pressed hard to find "that job" she really wanted. Home for Christmas, her dad, Art, encouraged her to be a little more flexible. "Honey, goals are important, and they keep you moving forward in the challenges of life, but God doesn't want your goals to take over your life. If you set things in cement, you're going to be disappointed. The picture you imagine for your life is never exactly as you see it now."

"You're right, Dad. I've been pressing in my direction and have allowed little time to hear what God wants. I will take some time during the Christmas break to allow God to help me set the right goals. I want His purpose and plan—not mine. Thanks for the reminder."

As I set goals and dream dreams,
give me wisdom so that all I do is in proper
alignment with Your plans for me. Amen.

This Christmas, God Wants You to Know...

THE BLESSING IS YOURS

The blessing of the LORD, it maketh rich,
and he addeth no sorrow with it.
PROVERBS 10:22 KJV

*E*lizabeth watched her young children scramble into the living room Christmas morning and assemble excitedly next to the Christmas tree. Their eyes scanned the Christmas name tags on each gift, trying to figure out which presents belonged to them. They were anxious for Mom to direct them, as they each would take turns opening their gifts.

She tried to hold on to the pleasure of being able to indulge a little this year in giving her children gifts. The anticipation of the look on their faces compelled her to shop for as many of the items on their individual lists as she could.

Just as Elizabeth loved giving gifts to her children, she recognized in that moment that God loved to pour blessings out on His children, too. Just as each of her children knew the gift with their names on it was theirs to open, hold, and enjoy—God had given her many blessings of love, comfort, joy, encouragement, and genuine care, poured out to her through friends and family members.

What blessings has God poured out into your life today? Consider that the greatest gift of all was His expression of love for you in sending His Son, Jesus, so you could have an eternal relationship with Him.

God, thank You for the blessings You pour out
freely on my life. Amen.

This Christmas, God Wants You to Know. . .

NO ONE CAN STEAL THE MUSIC HE PUT WITHIN YOU

He also brought me up out of a horrible pit, out of the miry clay,
and set my feet upon a rock, and established my steps.
He has put a new song in my mouth—Praise to our God;
many will see it and fear, and will trust in the LORD.
PSALM 40:2–3 NKJV

The trek to a new state, new city, new job, and new school left Bree feeling defeated. So many of the things she had put in place had come undone at the last minute. She called her girlfriend Tamara back home to vent a little.

"I had it all worked out. Now, I'm not sure if my student housing will be close enough to my new job. I didn't want the added gas expense of driving to work. And I don't know where the money will come from for my books since I won't get my first paycheck for two weeks."

"Oh, I'm sorry you're disappointed, Bree," Tamara chirped on the phone. "But you know God will take care of this—and then some."

"You're right," Bree responded. "I won't let the circumstances steal my song. I know this is where God wants me to be. I just need to relax and trust God. He always comes through." Bree hung up the phone and began to sing one of her favorite praise songs.

Today I choose joy.
I will sing the song You put in my heart.
I refuse to let my circumstances determine my attitude. Amen.

This Christmas, God Wants You to Know. . .

HE IS NOT ANGRY WITH YOU

Long ago the LORD said to Israel:
"I have loved you, my people, with an everlasting love.
With unfailing love I have drawn you to myself."
JEREMIAH 31:3 NLT

Cindie wrote on her Facebook page, "I must have done something wrong and made God mad. Dad is back in the hospital." Her friend and mentor, Shelley, saw her post and texted, I'M ON MY WAY.

When Shelley reached the waiting room, Cindie told her what had happened. Her father had been in and out of the hospital for most of the fall. But in anticipation of Christmas and being with family, he had followed the doctor's instructions and had been home the entire month of December. . .until now. "I've prayed and asked God to keep Dad healthy. I don't know what I did wrong, but I must have done something," Cindie cried.

Shelley put her arm around Cindie. "It's nothing you did or didn't do. God is not angry with you. He is not a big judge sitting in heaven waiting for you to mess up so He can punish you. He is love. Everything He does is out of love for you. We have challenges in this life, and we have His promise that we can overcome them by faith. It doesn't mean that things turn out exactly like we want. But God's desire is always to do good in your life."

Thank You for Your unconditional love. Help me to see that
Your plans for me are always good. Amen.

This Christmas, God Wants You to Know. . .

It's a Step of Faith

For we walk by faith, not by sight.
2 Corinthians 5:7 esv

Christmas wasn't really Christmas anymore at Madalyn's house. Her children were practically grown although they were both still in college. The last four years she had worked for a retail company that required staff to work the entire month of December.

With her family several thousand miles away, and her unable to travel, it wasn't a special celebration anymore. It was still about the Savior, but missing the joy of sharing it with her family left her with a hole in her heart. Last year her children had shared how her job "ruins Christmas" for everyone. She began to ask the Lord about this in her prayer time as Christmas approached.

After months of prayer, she felt that she should resign her position and trust God to open the next season of her professional life. The day she turned in her resignation, she made flight reservations for her children to all be home together for Christmas.

Also that day she received an e-mail from a former colleague asking if she'd be interested in taking some part-time work. Madalyn was thrilled. She had taken a step of faith, and the income from the part-time job would cover two-thirds of what her salary was with her company. As she continued to trust God, more opportunities opened to fully supplement her old salary.

Lord, show me when it's time to take that next step of faith,
and give me courage to do it. Amen.

This Christmas, God Wants You to Know. . .

You Can Walk on Water

*Thus says the LORD, who gives the sun for light by day
and the fixed order of the moon and the stars for
light by night, who stirs up the sea so that its
waves roar—the LORD of hosts is his name.*
JEREMIAH 31:35 ESV

*D*ebbie's mind raced. It was a cold and rainy Christmas Eve. The fog hung heavy out in front of her headlights. It didn't feel like Christmas to her. Her car had become a place of prayer. "Oh, God," she said, sighing. "You know everything I'm going through. My heart hurts. I want to hold my breath, hoping the storm will just wash away."

She turned on the radio in her car. The lyrics playing penetrated her heart: "Wonderful Jesus, I need Thee, Out in the storm and the strife, Oft it has seemed I was sinking, Tossed on the ocean of life. . . . Speak to my heart in the tempest, Whispering softly, 'Be still.' "[3]

She sang the song as a prayer. As the song ended, she felt her faith rise. Suddenly, she saw herself lifted above her circumstance. By His power she believed she could walk on water in the midst of it all.

*Father, let the sound of crashing waves fall away
as I look to You and walk on water in
the midst of the storm. Amen.*

---

3 Manie P. Ferguson, "Christ in the Storm," 1904.

This Christmas, God Wants You to Know. . .

HIS TIMING IS PERFECT

*Trust in the Lord and do good; dwell in the land
and enjoy safe pasture. Take delight in the Lord,
and he will give you the desires of your heart.*
PSALM 37:3–4 NIV

Camille was going to school and looking for a new job. She was close to completing her bachelor's degree and felt confident God had called her to fill a particular position at the organization of her dreams. But when she didn't get the job after three interviews, she was extremely disappointed.

She questioned her motives and whether she had heard from God. She had been certain that was the place God wanted her to work. Instead, she took another job at a "less-than-ideal" location. She learned a lot from her new boss about leadership. She graduated with her degree and began to move up within the company.

Still, she felt a tug in her heart. There was something about the company that hadn't hired her. She continued to ask the Lord about it but didn't really get any answers. Three years later, news came of a merge. Her current company had been purchased by the company she always dreamed of working for. As the transition began to happen, the new owners identified her as a candidate for leadership in the new organizational structure. Her heart leaped. She *had* heard God but just needed to wait for His timing.

*Lead me and I will follow. Show me the steps You have
ordered for me in Your perfect time. Amen.*

This Christmas, God Wants You to Know. . .

JESUS IS THE ONE TO FOLLOW

For to this you were called, because Christ also suffered for us,
leaving us an example, that you should follow His steps.
1 PETER 2:21 NKJV

The baby born in a manger that first Christmas Day was God's Son sent to earth as man. Mary, His mother, must have looked at Him as a small child with wonder, as He desired to learn the scriptures and understand God and His ways.

He grew in wisdom and stature, and as an adult, became the example to follow. Through the pages of the Bible, Jesus' words and actions are recorded. His life reveals the way to live that brings pleasure to the heavenly Father. He demonstrated how to interact with the Father, and with others.

The old saying "Like father, like son" is apparent in Jesus. He lived in obedience to His Father. Several times, even in His last days on earth, He stepped away to a quiet place to pray and maintain His connection to the heart with the Father. He knew God through prayer, worship, and His words in scripture.

When you come to know God, through the salvation experience, you can experience unity with God as Jesus did. His example will provide a clear picture of how to know the Father in Spirit and in truth.

Lord, as I learn more about the life of Jesus,
may I live my life in a way that pleases You. Amen.

83

This Christmas, God Wants You to Know. . .

YOUR STRENGTH IS IN HIM

David recovered everything the Amalekites had taken, including his
two wives. Nothing was missing: young or old, boy or girl,
plunder or anything else they had taken. David brought everything back.
1 SAMUEL 30:18–19 NIV

*F*irst Samuel 30 gives an account of a raid the enemy made on David's home in Ziklag, while David and his mighty men were gone. When they returned, they found their homes burned and their wives and children taken. The men were grief stricken and talked about stoning David, their leader. David knew his strength was in the Lord. He asked the Lord what to do—"Should I go after them?" And the Lord replied, instructing David to pursue the enemy with the promise that he would recover all.

He could have wallowed in his grief at the loss of his family. He could have given up and let the men stone him to death, but instead, he looked to the Lord for strength to get through this horrific circumstance he found himself and his entire army in. He stopped in the midst of all the chaos going on around him and said, "Lord, what input do You have on this situation?"

David believed God and followed His command. He found all that had been taken from him—his family and all of his possessions—because he asked God what to do and followed through.

Lord, in the midst of chaos, remind me that You are my
strength. I will always find my answers in You. Amen.

This Christmas, God Wants You to Know. . .

YOUR ADULT CHILDREN STILL NEED YOU

*This day I call the heavens and the earth as witnesses against you
that I have set before you life and death, blessings and curses.
Now choose life, so that you and your children may live.*
DEUTERONOMY 30:19 NIV

A senior in high school, Leah no longer wanted the caregiver, problem-solver, or finder-of-all-lost-things mom that Melissa had been for her up until a few years ago. Melissa felt like she was the thing that was now lost—and wasn't sure she could find the new identity of who she needed to become in this new relationship with her daughter, who would soon be an adult.

Melissa spent time in prayer asking the Lord for direction. She felt like she shouldn't offer an opinion about Leah's life choices unless she was asked. And then she tried to give a casual response with an inferred "the final decision is yours."

The first morning of Christmas break, Melissa felt a calm as the Lord spoke to her heart. "Don't you know I love Leah even more than you do? You have trained her well. Now trust Me to work in her life as I have done in yours."

Melissa felt a relief as she suddenly felt herself slip into place in a new relationship with her daughter. She was able to let go, recognizing that her daughter had always rested in the arms of her heavenly Father.

*As my children become adults,
teach me how to transition to my new role in their lives.
Thank You, Father. Amen.*

This Christmas, God Wants You to Know. . .

A GIFT FROM THE FORGOTTEN FATHER OF CHRISTMAS

*Because Mary's husband, Joseph, was a good man, he did not want
to disgrace her in public, so he planned to divorce her secretly.
While Joseph thought about these things, an angel of the Lord came
to him in a dream. The angel said, "Joseph, descendant of David,
don't be afraid to take Mary as your wife,
because the baby in her is from the Holy Spirit."*
MATTHEW 1:19–20 NCV

Often Joseph—the forgotten father of Christmas—is
an overlooked member of the Christmas story. Like Mary,
he was chosen. He released his hopes and dreams for the
future to allow God's plan to succeed. He made a decision to
believe that his fiancée had not been with another man, but
the child within her was placed within her by God.

Imagine the impact of how such a crisis—finding his fiancée with child—put him at a place in which he needed divine
direction. His relationship with God and with Mary was about
to be tested. His actions spoke louder than words. He determined that the things within his heart were more important
than the things going on around him. He embraced the angel's
words and willingly waited until God's child was born before
knowing Mary physically as her husband.

He let go of what he wanted and chose to live his life on
God's terms.

*Life doesn't always turn out the way I dreamed. Help me to
let go of what I want so I can embrace Your purpose. Amen.*

This Christmas, God Wants You to Know. . .

HE IS FULL OF MERCY

Let us then approach God's throne of grace with confidence,
so that we may receive mercy and find grace
to help us in our time of need.
HEBREWS 4:16 NIV

Gretchen and her brother, Dale, had spent the last two weeks moving their mother into her own apartment after selling their childhood home. Emotions were running high. Tired and hungry, they began going through the final few boxes of the things from the attic. When Gretchen offered to fix them some sandwiches, Dale snapped at her. "I want to get this done!" His words fell hard and painfully into her heart, but she remained silent.

Half an hour passed in silence, and then Dale took a deep breath. "Gretchen, I'm sorry. It feels like we're getting rid of Mom and Dad as we go through this stuff. And with Dad already gone, it just brings up the pain of his death. It's not an excuse. I just want to say I am sorry."

"I forgive you," Gretchen replied softly.

"So, you're not going to give me a hard time like you normally do when I'm a jerk?" he asked.

"No," she said. "There are times when I need mercy in my life. I believe if I give it out, it will come back to me."

Dale walked over and gave her a hug. "Thanks, sis! Now let's go get some lunch."

I find it hard to show mercy, especially when someone has wronged me. Help me to extend mercy to others. Amen.

This Christmas, God Wants You to Know. . .

JOY IS YOUR DECISION

"A woman, when she is in labor, has sorrow because her hour has come; but as soon as she has given birth to the child, she no longer remembers the anguish, for joy that a human being has been born into the world. Therefore you now have sorrow; but I will see you again and your heart will rejoice, and your joy no one will take from you."
JOHN 16:21–22 NKJV

Christmas is a season that exudes joy and celebration, but often it is lost in the midst of conflict—someone takes your parking place at the shopping mall. Another person cuts in front of you at the checkout stand. Maybe it's a deeper issue—the death of a loved one, financial difficulty, or relationships gone awry.

Circumstances want to crowd your mind and stop joy from happening in your heart. Conflict happens, but it's all about how you handle the encounter. Don't let conflict steal your Christmas. With His joy, you can respond in love and work through your differences. Joy is an inner dynamic that transforms you and redefines the circumstances. It doesn't deny what's going on but allows you to enjoy life in spite of what is going on.

You don't have to feel the joy before you respond with it. Don't depend on your circumstances to bring you joy—instead, rejoice first.

I have decided to live in joy today. I refuse to let my circumstances steal my joy because my joy comes from You. Amen.

This Christmas, God Wants You to Know. . .

THE WONDER OF WORSHIP

*About midnight Paul and Silas were praying
and singing songs to God as the other prisoners listened.
Suddenly, there was a strong earthquake that shook the foundation
of the jail. Then all the doors of the jail broke open,
and all the prisoners were freed from their chains.*
ACTS 16:25–26 NCV

*L*eslie loved the candlelight worship service her church hosted each Christmas Eve on the steps of the town hall. She bundled up tight—she zipped her coat, tied her hood, wrapped her scarf, and then pulled her gloves on a little tighter. She watched her breath escape her lips into the freezing night air.

Silently and reverently she got in line to receive her candle and then walked quietly to the steps where others were gathered. The singing had already started. She wondered if what she was feeling was in any way similar to what the shepherds and wise men felt the night her Savior was born.

As the group lifted their voices in praise, she felt the worries that threated to steal her joy lift. She thought of Paul and Silas singing praises that broke open the jail that was holding them captive. *That is the wonder of worship,* Leslie thought. *Worship opens my heart to God and provides a place where I am able to pour hope and freedom into my spirit.*

*Lord, when my heart is overwhelmed with the concerns of
the day, remind me that worship brings hope and freedom.
Amen.*

This Christmas, God Wants You to Know. . .

He Has Heard Your Request

*"Thus the Lord has dealt with me, in the days when
He looked on me, to take away my reproach among people."*
LUKE 1:25 NKJV

*T*essa picked up her phone and texted her best friend, Marissa: I NEED YOU. CAN YOU COME OVER RIGHT AWAY? Minutes later, Tessa heard Marissa's car in the driveway and opened the front door. Before her feet reached the threshold, Tessa broke down and fell into Marissa's arms.

Marissa slowly led her back into the house where they sat down on the couch. "He walked out," Tessa sobbed. "He found someone else." There were no more words. Marissa just held her as Tessa grieved the loss of her marriage.

Years passed, and Tessa remained faithful to allow God to heal her broken heart. She learned to worship Him through her pain and asked God to bring someone into her life—when the timing was right—who would love her completely as He meant for her to be loved.

Then suddenly, the time was right and God began to open the door to all that she had longed for. She was introduced to a new client of Marissa's at a Christmas party. "He asked me if it would be okay for me to give him your phone number," Marissa whispered to Tessa. Tessa blushed and nodded yes. Within the year, the two were happily married.

*Thank You, Lord, for being there when my hope is
shattered and for hearing my request. Amen.*

This Christmas, God Wants You to Know. . .

YOU ARE HIS WITNESS

In the same way, encourage the young men to live wisely.
And you yourself must be an example to them by doing good works
of every kind. Let everything you do reflect the integrity
and seriousness of your teaching.
TITUS 2:6–7 NLT

Stephanie had a coworker who proved more difficult to work with than any person she had ever met. "Nathan was angry, bitter, hurt, jealous, and bent on seeing me fail in every aspect of my career," she told her best friend, Gail. "Sometimes I would be so upset with him that I would go to the bathroom and cry. And when I prayed, I didn't like what God seemed to say about the situation."

"What did God say?" Gail asked.

"He wants me to love this person and, at first, I really didn't think I could. Then one day in the bathroom, I told God, 'Okay! I'm going to love Nathan no matter what!' "

"So, what changed?" Gail asked.

"I asked God to help me to see Nathan with His love," Stephanie continued. "Every time Nathan was nasty, I'd go in the bathroom, look in the mirror, and say, 'I will love him no matter what!' Amazingly, I find myself truly caring about him. I want him to see God's love in me. And I think, slowly, his heart is softening toward me."

The world is watching. God desires for you to demonstrate His goodness and love.

Let me be an example of Your love to all who see me. Amen.

This Christmas, God Wants You to Know. . .

YOU ARE WHAT YOU EAT—SPIRITUALLY

For the weapons of our warfare are not carnal but mighty in God for
pulling down strongholds, casting down arguments and every high
thing that exalts itself against the knowledge of God, bringing every
thought into captivity to the obedience of Christ.

2 CORINTHIANS 10:4–5 NKJV

*M*ost have a challenge when it comes to eating sweets
at Christmas. In the cheer of the holiday, you celebrate with
the delicious and wonderful things that delight your taste
buds. The old adage "You are what you eat" is true spiritually
as well. What you allow in through your eyes, ears, and
mouth has an impact on your thoughts. Just like food high
in nutrition promotes health in your body, the thoughts you
allow in your mind contribute to the welfare of your spirit.

Words and images that oppose God's Word can pollute
your mind. They can become poison and eventually steal
the very purpose God has for your life. Negative words like
"You'll never amount to anything; you're a nobody" tear
down your confidence in who you are in Christ just as "You
can do all things through Christ" builds your confidence.

As you make a conscious effort to feed your spirit
with the right words, sights, and sounds, you will grow and
develop your spirit. You can choose what goes in and out of
your mind and heart today.

I take every thought that exalts itself against God
and throw it out with the trash today! Amen.

This Christmas, God Wants You to Know. . .

HE IS EVERYTHING GOOD

Taste and see that the LORD is good.
Oh, the joys of those who take refuge in him!
PSALM 34:8 NLT

Three-year-old Dillon was still sitting at the kitchen table after the rest of the family had finished their meal. He refused to taste the green peas his mother, Stella, had put on his plate. "You don't have to eat them if you don't like them," she told him, "but you have to taste them. You can't leave the table until you at least take one bite." So he sat there.

His father, Russell, came in to provide a little courage. "Buddy, just one bite. That's all we're asking." Dillon stalled as he pushed the handle of his fork like a little race car around and around his plate, making motor noises.

"Dad," Dillon asked, keeping his eyes on his fork, "did God make peas?"

Russell looked quizzically at his son, wondering where he was going with this one. "Yes," he said.

"Well, my Sunday school teacher said that God made everything good. So if He made it, then it's supposed to be good."

Russell smiled at his logic. "Well, sometimes. . . ," he began to explain, but it was too late. Dillon had scooped a spoonful of peas into his mouth and started to chew. He slid off the chair and opened his mouth to show his dad he'd swallowed.

"Not bad," he reported.

Each day I learn to trust You more,
as I discover just how good You really are. Amen.

This Christmas, God Wants You to Know. . .

He Works the Night Shift

"Because of the tender mercy of our God, whereby the sunrise shall visit us from on high to give light to those who sit in darkness and in the shadow of death, to guide our feet into the way of peace."
Luke 1:78–79 esv

Justin couldn't sleep. He stared into the darkness, and fear gripped his heart. He heard that taunting voice in his head. *Guess who won't have Christmas this year? Your wife is going to die.* He fought to push the voice out, but his fear was real. Thoughts and images of a life without her crept into his mind. He tried to stir up his faith—but it didn't come. Thankfully, he knew many others were praying.

For the past week, he had lived at the hospital. His wife, Miranda, had gone into the hospital for a routine hysterectomy, but they found much more than they expected. Infection had set in, and it was life threatening. She had become unresponsive.

Suddenly, his phone rang and startled him. It was his wife's night nurse. "I have good news. Your wife is awake and responsive. Her white cell count is up, and she has opened her eyes."

It can be so hard when you can't see the light. If you are in a dark season, there is hope—God works the night shift.

⁓

Thank You, God, that You are not limited by the night. I can count on You to be with me even when I can't see the light. Amen.

This Christmas, God Wants You to Know. . .

LOVE SERVES AS YOUR FILTER

But we have the true hope that comes from being made
right with God, and by the Spirit we wait eagerly for this hope.
When we are in Christ Jesus, it is not important if we are
circumcised or not. The important thing is faith—
the kind of faith that works through love.
GALATIANS 5:5–6 NCV

*D*anielle brought the two gallons of milk and set them in the fridge. "Mom," she said. "Tell me about Christmas when you were a little girl." Vivian looked at her daughter after setting the rest of the groceries on the counter.

"Well, one thing I loved about Christmas at my grandparents' house was the way they did things back then and the things I learned. My grandparents had cows that provided them with milk. In the winter, I would put on my snow boots, bundle up, and traipse out to the barn behind my grandfather. I'd watch him milk the cow; then we'd bring the warm milk in and set it on the counter. My grandmother would use a cloth as a filter to strain the milk, making it clean for us to drink."

"So," Danielle inquired, "what did you learn?"

Vivian replied, "It helped me to see that the love of God serves as a filter for our faith. Faith works by love. Because we are in Christ, we have a filter with which to see the world with the eyes of faith."

Let love be the filter by which my faith is
activated in all things. Amen.

95

This Christmas, God Wants You to Know. . .

YOU ARE HIS CHOICE FOR SOMETHING SIGNIFICANT

And her husband Joseph, being a just man and unwilling to put her to shame, resolved to divorce her quietly. But as he considered these things, behold, an angel of the Lord appeared to him in a dream, saying, "Joseph, son of David, do not fear to take Mary as your wife, for that which is conceived in her is from the Holy Spirit."

MATTHEW 1:19–20 ESV

Joseph was chosen to serve as a father figure to God's Son, Jesus, because of his character. He was willing to obey God, no matter the cost. The woman he loved was pregnant, and he knew he was not the father of her child. Imagine the thoughts running through his head.

Then God sent an angel to confirm that the baby was the Messiah and it was God's desire for Joseph to raise the child as his own. Joseph did exactly what God instructed him to do. He forfeited his dreams for God's plans. He was willing to be misunderstood and falsely judged.

Christmas is about a man willing to surrender everything, and in the process, he discovered he was God's choice to raise God's one and only Son. Like Joseph, can God trust you to be the righteous man or woman He needs in order to bring about His plans today?

Father, Help me to choose Your plans over my own desires. Show me Your way so that I may be Your choice for something significant. Amen.

This Christmas, God Wants You to Know. . .

YOUR GIFT WILL MAKE A WAY FOR YOU

A man's gift makes room for him, and brings him before great men.
PROVERBS 18:16 NKJV

Kara and Jan were enjoying a day together as they shopped for the last few Christmas gifts on their lists. Suddenly, a darling little girl about six years old caught their attention. "Sometimes when I see a small child, I try to imagine the potential God put inside of them," Kara remarked. "Growing up, I dreamed that someday I would become a writer. I was captured by the feeling of ink flowing out and filling up the pages with each small stroke of my hand."

"But you *are* a writer," Jan stated.

"Yes, but it didn't look like my dream was going to come true. I got married, quit college, and buried my desire to put words onto paper. Years passed, and God put His plan in motion. Through a series of promotions at different companies, God opened the door for me to write again. I suddenly realized that the dream was still within me."

"Wow," Jan exclaimed. "You gave up and God brought it back around."

"Yes," Kara admitted, "I'm living proof that your gift will make a way for you."

When you trust God to take your life and do with it what He purposed, He'll make your dreams a reality in His time. Just trust Him!

*Revive the dreams You put within me, God.
Only You have the power to restore them. Amen.*

This Christmas, God Wants You to Know. . .

His Ways Are Perfect—Even When People Aren't

"God's way is perfect. All the Lord's promises prove true.
He is a shield for all who look to him for protection."
2 Samuel 22:31 nlt

Miranda heard the door slam hard as her twenty-one-year-old son, Kyle, walked into the house. She knew immediately something was wrong because his normally optimistic, easygoing attitude remained well hidden behind the scowl on his face as he walked into the kitchen. "Hi, honey," she said. "Do you want to talk about it?"

"I had one of those days—people are so frustrating. It makes me wonder how God can be so merciful and gracious," Kyle complained.

"The world is so completely opposite of what God desires from us—people are so mean, hurtful, and spiteful sometimes. Thankfully, you know God and His ways. You can rely on Him and pray for those who don't know Him. He'll give you wisdom and discernment regarding each situation. His ways are perfect, and as you respond to others in His love, He will give you His very best."

Kyle smiled. "Yeah! I know. I feel better after acknowledging my feelings about it. You always encourage me to choose His ways. Thanks, Mom!"

Give me grace for others, Lord, when I feel a lack
of justice in how others treat me. Let me respond
with wisdom and Your perfect peace! Amen.

This Christmas, God Wants You to Know. . .

HIS SPIRIT WANTS TO LEAD YOU

Therefore, if anyone is in Christ, the new creation has come:
The old has gone, the new is here.
2 CORINTHIANS 5:17 NIV

God's love and desire for relationship compelled Him to create humanity. God created us in His likeness—for our spirit to rule our mind, will, and emotions and to direct our bodies in what is right. When Adam and Eve disobeyed God's command, their relationship with God was severed. Their desire for knowledge led to the death of their spirits and to their reliance upon a physical knowledge—their physical senses told them what to feel and think. The physical and natural became dominant over the spirit.

Before you experienced relationship with Christ, your spirit man sat in darkness, allowing your physical senses to interpret your life for you. Once you accepted the sacrifice Jesus made to bring you back to God, His life and light immediately illuminated your spirit. Your spirit, full of new life, was ready to go to work, but the habit of allowing your senses to lead you caused conflict in you. As a new Spirit-led creation, your spirit wants to lead.

The apostle Paul said you are a new creature. The old person—ruled by the physical world—dies, and you become alive in Christ to forever be led by your spirit man.

I chose to be Spirit led today. Help me to choose Your will and Your way in everything I do. Amen.

This Christmas, God Wants You to Know. . .

YOU'RE CLOSER THAN YOU THINK

And behold, the star that they had seen when it rose went before them until it came to rest over the place where the child was.
MATTHEW 2:9 ESV

A woman came forward during an altar call and was visibly moved by the presence and power of God. The minister asked her what happened. The new believer replied, "I don't even know exactly how I got down here to the front. I've been looking for something all my life. This evening, I was driving by your church and the next thing I know I'm standing here, finding Christ."

That first Christmas, the wise men saw a star. They had been on a thousand-mile journey. They were looking for the King of the Jews, who had been born. Someone said, "We'll take you to King Herod; he's our king." And as soon as they walked into the throne room they knew—that was not the king—not the one they were searching for, anyway. They knew they were looking for a baby—not a man.

Have you ever been on a journey that you just knew God told you to take, and you're almost there but you feel like you missed it? Perhaps the wise men didn't know that Bethlehem is four short miles from Jerusalem. God wants you to go all the way to Bethlehem; don't stop short of your answer. You are closer to the answer than you think.

Lord, give me the courage to go the distance and discover my destiny! Amen.

This Christmas, God Wants You to Know. . .

HE KNOWS THE END FROM THE BEGINNING

"For I am God, and there is no other; I am God,
and there is none like me, declaring the end from the beginning
and from ancient times things not yet done, saying, 'My counsel
shall stand, and I will accomplish all my purpose.'"
ISAIAH 46:9–10 ESV

*D*ayna reflected on the day she sat in the car, heartbroken, while her daughter, Rebecca, went into the counseling center alone. She had offered to go with her for moral support, but Rebecca had refused. "It's my mess, Mom," she said. "I'll clean it up."

If only it were that simple, Dayna had thought. When Rebecca admitted she had a serious drug addiction, she thought her heart—for a moment—had turned to stone. She had gone completely numb, with the exception of the weight of her heart resting hard within her chest, pressing in so hard, suffocating her. There were no words, and thankfully, Rebecca had not expected any.

Now three years later, Rebecca served as a missionary to elementary students in the inner cities. Such a painful experience positioned her heart to make a difference in the lives of others. Dayna could see that she was happy and willing to go wherever God would send her.

He knows what choices you will make before you make them and what your destiny will bring.

Lord, use me. I want to fulfill the destiny You put within me
and complete my purpose so I may please You. Amen.

This Christmas, God Wants You to Know. . .

YOU CAN EXPERIENCE CHRISTMAS EVERY DAY

Don't just pretend to love others. Really love them. Hate what is wrong. Hold tightly to what is good. Love each other with genuine affection, and take delight in honoring each other.

ROMANS 12:9–10 NLT

Dale Evans said, "Christmas, my child, is love in action. Every time we love, every time we give, it's Christmas."

Many things demonstrate a picture of love: a locket around your neck, a ring on your finger. Love is invincible in the face of death as a woman stands next to the bed of the one she married more than sixty years ago, holding his hand, caressing his face, cradling his head in her hands, and kissing him as he leaves this earth for heaven.

Passion laughs at the terrors of hell. The fire of love stops at nothing—it sweeps everything before it. Flood waters can't drown love, and torrents of rain can't put it out. Love can't be bought; love can't be sold—it's not to be found in the marketplace.

Love in action is stronger than death. It is so priceless that even the richest of all kingdoms cannot purchase it for any price. It is a gift from God and you are encouraged to live it completely and unrestrained. You can experience Christmas every day as you look into your heart and convey the true meaning of God's ultimate gift to others.

I pray I may bring glory to You each day, as I choose to share the love of Christmas with others. Amen.

This Christmas, God Wants You to Know. . .

It's Time to Look Up

"Then people will see the Son of Man coming in a cloud
with power and great glory. When these things begin to happen,
look up and hold your heads high, because the time
when God will free you is near!"
LUKE 21:27–28 NCV

When Holly and Jeff decided to get married, he told her he didn't want any secrets between them and then shared that he had a daughter, who had been given up for adoption. He was still in high school when she was born, but it was his hope that someday his daughter would look for him and they would be reunited.

"Sometimes it's the unexpected events in life that help us understand the most," Holly commented to her friend Kenna regarding Jeff's dream of reconnecting with his daughter. "Like, in one day, everything changed for my entire family. We have a daughter, our sons have an older sister, and we have a son-in-law and grandson. And on top of it all, she wants to be a part of our lives, a part of our family."

Kenna smiled. "I am so happy for all of you. Christmas looks completely different now for all of you."

"Yes," Holly cheered. "Our lives will never be the same. For years we wondered if this day would ever come and then suddenly, Jeff looked up and she was reaching out to him."

Help me to look up and see the blessings You've put in my life;
I don't want to miss a single one. Amen.

This Christmas, God Wants You to Know. . .

HE WILL MEET YOU WHERE YOU ARE

For by grace you have been saved through faith.
And this is not your own doing; it is the gift of God,
not a result of works, so that no one may boast.
EPHESIANS 2:8–9 ESV

Maude and Leah connected one Sunday morning at church. Maude noticed Leah sitting in the row in front of her all by herself, and so Maude introduced herself. The two ladies connected instantly. It was one of those divine connections.

The two ladies met every week at a coffee shop or for lunch at one of their favorite places. Leah was discouraged. She had lost her job, her marriage was a wreck, and Leah's side of the conversation had become negative almost every time the two got together. Finally Maude decided to offer some truth in love.

"Even as Christians, we have stuff in our lives, Leah," Maude said. "God's grace has broken the power of sin in your life and you have freedom. It's up to you to decide how you live in that freedom. All the things you are frustrated about were there before you knew God. Give Him some time and space to work things out."

"So you're saying give myself some grace and give God some space to help me grow in the direction God wants me to go—from here!"

Maude smiled. "You got it!"

I am so thankful that You meet me where I am. I don't have to get all cleaned up before I can experience Your love or grace. Amen.

This Christmas, God Wants You to Know. . .

LOVE IS WHAT MATTERS

If anyone claims, "I am living in the light," but hates a Christian
brother or sister, that person is still living in darkness.
Anyone who loves another brother or sister is living
in the light and does not cause others to stumble.
1 JOHN 2:9–10 NLT

*H*ave you ever had one of those arguments where someone *just had to be right*? When you get caught in the trap of having to be right at all costs, it can damage or even destroy your relationship with others. In light of a failed relationship, being the one who is right becomes pointless.

Perhaps you've gone away thinking they didn't "get it" when they got a clear message—you felt the relationship was less important than your point—or your pride. Ultimately, love is all that matters. God's love doesn't cause pain but strives to miss hurt altogether.

The harsh truth is if you dismiss love, you've missed God's plan, no matter how right you think you are. As you see others through the eyes of love, you can change the way you respond to them. God is love. In a desire to respond to love the way He desires, ask yourself the question: Does my body language, tone, and character reflect love—God's character?

Let Your love flow out of me toward others,
just as You have poured Your love out on me. Amen.

This Christmas, God Wants You to Know. . .

His Presence Will Go with You

And he said, "My presence will go with you,
and I will give you rest."
EXODUS 33:14 ESV

*N*atalie was nervous about the move to the air force base with all four children. They had never lived on base before while her husband, Carter, was deployed. With the convenience of home school, she'd always stayed with her parents. With her oldest, Tyler, in high school, they had promised him he could go to public school, and the Academy in Colorado Springs had an excellent high school.

Carter noticed her wrinkled forehead. "Honey, it's going to be okay. The kids are older now, and it will be a little easier. I have three months before I deploy, so we'll find a good church home to get settled, and we will make great friends on base. With your parents being willing to come for a month at Christmas, I believe it'll make things less stressful."

"You are right on all accounts," Natalie said. "I can't find my Israel Houghton CD. You know the one with the song, 'Your Presence Is Heaven to Me.' That song has gotten me through so many nights when you were away. The words speak to my heart, and I feel the presence of God comfort me no matter where I am. I wanted to have it in the car with me as we make the move to our new place."

Thank You, Father, for Your presence. No matter where I go,
Your presence always goes with me. Amen.

This Christmas, God Wants You to Know. . .

HE WILL GIVE YOU STRENGTH AND PEACE

The LORD gives strength to his people;
the LORD blesses his people with peace.
PSALM 29:11 NIV

*E*lizabeth didn't want to think about Christmas with her family. She and her husband went on a cruise during Thanksgiving so she didn't have to deal with the realization that her mother would never be at a family function again.

Her mother had always been healthy, so for her to die unexpectedly of a heart attack at sixty-three was something the whole family had a hard time with. Her mother had been the matriarch of the family, the one who got everyone together for any holiday, and now everyone was looking to Elizabeth.

Since her mother's death, she had skipped her time with God. She knew at some point she would have to talk to Him, but she wasn't ready. He seemed far away—as if she were on one island and He were on another, with a foggy mist separating them.

She noticed her husband had pulled the Christmas tree and boxes of decorations into the living room. "God, I don't think I can do this," she said as she fell onto the couch. Suddenly, she felt His voice in her heart: *"I'm here to help; experience My peace."* His voice was like a gust of wind that blew the fog between them away, and she felt His presence. There was no longer distance between them.

When my heart is breaking, comfort me with Your peace
and fill me with Your strength. Amen.

This Christmas, God Wants You to Know. . .

He Desires for You to Be Well

*Beloved, I pray that you may prosper in all things
and be in health, just as your soul prospers.*
3 JOHN 1:2 NKJV

*O*nce again, Bart's health examination revealed what his wife, Jessica, had already expected—his sugar levels were up, and the doctor wanted to put him on medication. He was already taking medication to regulate his blood pressure, and he was only thirty-three years old. Whenever he was consistent with his diet and exercise, he was able to maintain a healthy weight and the medication was not necessary, but sugary sweets during the holidays left him unsuccessful in his promise to change his lifestyle.

Jessica tried not to say anything, but sometimes her concern about the situation got the best of her, and she pressed him about it. She feared his health would decline, leaving her to go on without him and raise their family alone. Finally, she realized there was nothing she could do to encourage him or help him. This was something he had to choose for himself.

She began to go to God in prayer about her concerns instead of trying to make her husband do what she thought was best for him. She studied the scriptures about healing in the Bible to help her pray for her husband and continue to give her concerns to God.

God, thank You for providing me with the opportunity to choose health. Give me the strength to choose wisely so I can experience health in every single area of my life. Amen.

This Christmas, God Wants You to Know...

IT'S YOUR CHOICE

To choose life is to love the LORD your God, obey him, and stay close to him. He is your life, and he will let you live many years in the land, the land he promised to give your ancestors Abraham, Isaac, and Jacob.

DEUTERONOMY 30:20 NCV

Dena held out the car keys to her sixteen-year-old daughter. Her heart was beating fast. This was the first time she'd allowed Nora to take the car on her own at night, but she knew it was time. "There is a lot of traffic out this weekend with all the holiday shoppers. And the later it gets there is more of a chance for drunk drivers to be on the road...."

"Mom, I'll be fine," Nora offered. "I have taken driver's ed. I'm a good driver."

Dena nodded. "Yes, you're a really good driver." She hesitated. "But it's not just the driving. You are on your own, about to make decisions. We live each day making choices—life or death. I was just thinking about the choices I made as a young adult that took me into dangerous situations. It always started as a little thing, but then it grew, little by little, and I was waist deep in a mess before I knew it."

Nora's face softened. "Mom, don't worry; you have taught me well, and your prayers will see me through."

———

Today, in all I do, I choose life. Amen.

This Christmas, God Wants You to Know. . .

HE WILL BE YOUR HERO

"The LORD your God is in your midst, a mighty one who will save;
he will rejoice over you with gladness; he will quiet you by his love;
he will exult over you with loud singing."

ZEPHANIAH 3:17 ESV

*T*rish needed a hero. As a child she invited Jesus into her life, and for the most part, He remained a continuous friend. At eight or nine years old, while her parents fought, she would lie in her bed in the dark and talk to God. He was her safety, her hope, and her trust when the hurt in her home was too much too handle.

During her teen years, she admitted there were times when she just didn't include Him in things, but she knew He was always there. When she put herself in unsafe situations as a teenager and then realized the danger of her situation, God made a way of escape—every time.

Over the course of her life, God was there—reaching out, lifting her up, and pulling her out of every mess she found herself in—and celebrating with her in the great blessings He brought her way.

You may never understand the love God has for you. The love you feel from others cannot compare to the love God has for you. He is always with you, ready to defend you and save you. He is the greatest of heroes.

You are my hero. You are here with me, always reaching to
save me and bring me into Your loving arms. Amen.

This Christmas, God Wants You to Know. . .

He Works Behind the Scenes

So we fix our eyes not on what is seen, but on what is unseen,
since what is seen is temporary, but what is unseen is eternal.
2 Corinthians 4:18 niv

Dennis arrived early at the playhouse to handle lights and the curtain for his granddaughter's performance that night. He was a doer—he had to be busy doing something. Lending his time to something his children or grandchildren were involved in kept him connected to their lives and excited when they showed interest in the things he enjoyed—like theater.

As he tested a few things, he began to think about his life as a father and grandfather. Since it was difficult for him to be still, it was just natural for him to imagine God busy—always doing things behind the scenes in the lives of His children.

The Bible says He never slumbers or sleeps, Dennis thought, *so I believe He's doing something in my life all the time.* As he imagined the stagehands scurrying around behind the stage, accomplishing tasks most audience members never see, he wondered what God was doing in his life. As he spent time with God in prayer, he always felt an anticipation for the good things he was trusting God to do—in His own time—and in His own way.

I will be faithful to trust as I anticipate the next big reveal because of all You're doing behind the scenes in my life! Amen.

This Christmas, God Wants You to Know. . .

HE WILL BLESS YOU WITH A LONG LIFE

The fear of the LORD prolongs days,
but the years of the wicked will be shortened.
PROVERBS 10:27 NKJV

When Kacie had her first child, Collyn, he was the fifth living generation on her mother's paternal side. Collyn's great-great-grandmother was still living in her own home, sweeping her own front porch; her grandparents lived close enough to her that they offered to take care of Collyn when she went back to work.

Collyn followed his great-grandfather around the farm, trying his best to keep in step behind him. He mimicked his great-grandfather's actions, and as he grew, he discovered how they did things in "the old, old days," as he called it.

As Kacie, her sisters, and her cousins had their families, Christmas was a special time of the year as her grandparents shared stories of generations past. She loved that her children had a close family and had the opportunity to learn from several generations as they grew up.

When Collyn was in college, his great-grandfather closed his eyes on Christmas Eve at ninety-five years old and died. Collyn knew God had blessed his great-grandfather with a long life, much like his great-great-grandmother his mother had been close to, who had died at 105. His grandfather told him that was a legacy that he could be a part of, too.

Thank You for the blessing of a long life as I honor and respect You, giving You glory as I live my life for You. Amen.

This Christmas, God Wants You to Know. . .

YOU WERE BORN TO BELIEVE

*While He was still speaking, some came from the ruler of
the synagogue's house who said, "Your daughter is dead.
Why trouble the Teacher any further?" As soon as Jesus heard the
word that was spoken, He said to the ruler of the synagogue,
"Do not be afraid; only believe."*

MARK 5:35–36 NKJV

Sometimes I get so irritated with myself," Deborah complained to her sister, Dixie. "I've even told God, 'When I don't see it, I have to fight to believe it.' I know He's God and He has always made a way when I didn't see one."

Dixie smiled. "We learn that we can trust Him every time—especially in the hardest parts of life. Even when I thought it was over and the darkness had won, God shined His light into the situation at what felt like the last moment and delivered truth."

"I wish I could be the opposite—instead of having such a hard time believing, I could just believe," Deborah added. "It gets better. Each time I stretch my faith by believing more than I did the time before, my faith grows. Then the next time my faith goes further and the gap is less of a distance to the next level."

"Faith is like a developing muscle," Dixie agreed. "The more we use it, the stronger it grows."

*I was born to believe. Increase my faith as
I grow to the next level. Amen.*

This Christmas, God Wants You to Know. . .

YOU CAN LOVE EVEN THE MOST DIFFICULT PEOPLE

A gentle answer turns away wrath, but a harsh word stirs up anger.
The tongue of the wise adorns knowledge,
but the mouth of the fool gushes folly.
PROVERBS 15:1–2 NIV

"My mother can really push my buttons," Marta confessed to her coworker, Jim, after a phone call from her interrupted her workday. "I just don't know what to do sometimes. She's inconsiderate and selfish. Granted, she's had a difficult few years, but she oozes with negativity."

"No one is perfect, and you know," Jim encouraged, "God's Word undoubtedly reassures us to choose peace and guard our words." Marta frowned. "We all have difficult people in our lives. I've discovered I don't have to do this on my own. The Bible said that God's love is poured out in our hearts. We can respond with His love, which is limitless."

"So you're saying those times when I want to hang up the phone or give my mother a piece of my mind, I can let God's love flow? It's a choice?"

"Yes," Jim answered. "But it takes self-control and a lot of practice. I've learned to take a deep breath, count to ten, and listen to see what the Holy Spirit tells me to do next. It's the only way I can really choose to follow His example and respond with love."

Show me how to love those who bring challenges into my life today. Let them see Your love in me. Amen.

This Christmas, God Wants You to Know. . .

It's about Relationship

Jesus said to him, " 'You shall love the Lord your God with all your heart, with all your soul, and with all your mind.' This is the first and great commandment. And the second is like it: 'You shall love your neighbor as yourself.' "
MATTHEW 22:37–39 NKJV

Cookie came back to the dining room table, surprised to find all the cousins still sitting around the table. She had gone into the living room to check on the kids. They were all piled on top of one another, snuggled down in their sleeping bags near the fireplace with a Christmas movie on the TV.

"Reminds me of all of us when we were little," Cookie commented.

"Yeah," Mitch commented, "except we didn't have TV. Grandma would tell us story after story instead."

"I'm surprised to see you all still sitting here. I figured the guys would go into the game room and shoot some pool."

"No," A. J. replied, leaning back in his chair like he was a little kid again. "We haven't all been together in such a long time."

"Some of my most favorite memories are from the Christmases we spent together at Grandpa and Grandma's when we were little like that," Chris said. Then they began a long conversation of "remember when," each telling their favorite memory of Christmas when they were together.

Lord, thank You for the relationships I have with You and many others that I can share Christmas with. Amen.

This Christmas, God Wants You to Know. . .

YOU ARE HIS WITNESS IN THE EARTH

"But you will receive power when the Holy Spirit has come upon
you, and you will be my witnesses in Jerusalem and in all Judea
and Samaria, and to the end of the earth."
ACTS 1:8 ESV

Michael's job kept him away from the family more than he or Ella liked. She found herself doing more and more on her own. She worked to keep a joyful heart in the midst of this season in their life. "Someday," she told herself, "it won't be this way."

She pushed her grocery cart up and down the aisle with her toddler in the seat and her five-year-old "helping" her get the things she needed. She noticed a woman watching her, and she spoke up. "You have such patience with your son and such a joyful attitude in the midst of all these grouchy grocery shoppers. How do you do it?"

Ella smiled at the woman, hesitated for just a second, and then said softly, "It's not easy, but my joy comes from spending time each day with the Lord." Ella had learned that her job as a believer wasn't proclaiming the answer but inspiring the world to ask the question.

The woman smiled at Ella and said, "Thank you for sharing that with me. It encourages me that you are not afraid to speak up and be His witness."

Heavenly Father, fill me up with Your joy so that others
are inspired to ask about You. Amen.

This Christmas, God Wants You to Know. . .

He Will Carry You through the Storms

"But everyone who hears these sayings of Mine, and does not do them, will be like a foolish man who built his house on the sand: and the rain descended, the floods came, and the winds blew and beat on that house; and it fell. And great was its fall."
MATTHEW 7:26–27 NKJV

*A*lice was flying into Denver alone. The rest of her family had gone on ahead of her to start the Christmas celebrations early. Normally she loved to fly, but they had encountered some weather and the plane was bouncing all around. The captain's voice came on over the loudspeaker and said, "We've got to navigate through this big storm, and there is no going around it. Please sit down and buckle up."

She looked down and tightened her seat belt. *So glad I took my meds for nausea,* she thought. The man sitting in the aisle seat next to her said rather loudly, "Storms reveal what you are made of." She looked at him quizzically, and he continued, "You can be ready to face any storm as long as you have a sure foundation." Alice thought the man was odd but then realized he might be talking about the story Jesus told in the Bible of the wise man who built his house on a rock. Only the life built on God's plan survives the storm.

God, You are the captain of my flight.
Thank You for getting me through the storms. Amen.

This Christmas, God Wants You to Know...

JESUS CAME TO CHANGE YOUR STORY

But because of his great love for us, God, who is rich in mercy,
made us alive with Christ even when we were dead in
transgressions—it is by grace you have been saved.
EPHESIANS 2:4–5 NIV

You've seen them—the people on the highways with signs asking for help. Do you ever wonder about their story?" Nancy asked her friend Tiffany, who was sitting across from her in the coffee shop.

"Yes," Tiffany replied. "Sometimes I feel sorry for them; other times I wonder if it's all a scam and they're making more money that I am."

"The cardboard notes they hold tell a tiny portion of their story," Nancy replied. "We've all got a story—each story is a composite of all the events, relationships, and experiences—that shaped who we are today."

Tiffany set her coffee cup down. "Everyone has a story. So many stories are filled with heartache. So many have given up hope that their story could ever be any better."

"I am so thankful that Jesus came into my life and changed my story. I could have easily been one of those people holding a cardboard note on the road," Nancy admitted. "When I accepted Jesus, it's like He took my nightmare of a story, shredded it into tiny pieces, and gave me a new book where He had written a brand-new story for my life."

When I am tempted to get stuck with my old story,
remind me that I have a brand-new story to live. Amen.

This Christmas, God Wants You to Know. . .

THE POWER OF LETTING GO

"Do not judge others, and you will not be judged.
Do not condemn others, or it will all come back against you.
Forgive others, and you will be forgiven."
LUKE 6:37 NLT

At thirty-something Kaitlyn still struggled with her parents' divorce. She had pretended to be over the pain for such a long time that she had almost convinced herself it was true. Then, her brother Jeremiah's divorce brought the old suitcase of bad childhood memories that had lain hidden for years out of the attic.

A friend asked Kaitlyn to consider a grief-recovery class with her where she found the tools she needed to unpack the past. With each memory—good or bad—she found in her relationship with her father, she was able to give voice to her emotions and finally say the things she had left unsaid in her heart. The process took weeks and gave her an opportunity to finally let it all go.

She discovered freedom in forgiveness. She suddenly felt she was free from the prison that held her captive. She no longer felt anger when she thought of her father or his new family she had never been a part of.

Letting go, she was able to absolve her father from the consequences and allow all the offenses to pass through her heart without punishment. She discovered she was empowered to pardon as freely as God does.

You don't bring up yesterday's mistakes; instead,
You look to the future. My hope is in You! Amen.

This Christmas, God Wants You to Know. . .

PATIENCE WILL BRING HIS DESIRED RESULTS

Be still before the LORD and wait patiently for him;
fret not yourself over the one who prospers in his way,
over the man who carries out evil devices!
PSALM 37:7 ESV

At Christmastime, Marsha was right there with the kids in wanting to open Christmas presents. If she had her way, she would have most of the gifts out from under the tree and opened before Christmas morning ever arrived. And truth be told, a tree without gifts under it on Christmas morning is a sad sight. After years of this from their mother, even the children got on board with their dad, refusing to open gifts. They discovered that after they opened and played with all the gifts, the anticipation and excitement of Christmas morning was lost because of lack of patience.

This Christmas Marsha was determined to wait it out. She discovered a powerful scripture that spoke to her impatient heart. As Christmas grew near and presents were placed under the tree, she would turn her thoughts to Psalm 46:10: *"Be still and know that I am God."*

Christmas morning came, and not a single gift was opened early. She found the excitement and thrill of opening gifts waned in comparison to the peace and patience she had found as she kept her focus on the true reason for the season.

Patience takes faith. I know that only by Your power
am I able to wait as I keep my focus on You. Amen.

This Christmas, God Wants You to Know. . .

He Has a Better Plan

Depend on the Lord in whatever you do, and your plans will succeed.
PROVERBS 16:3 NCV

Stan and Kellie were planners. They had set their goals and laid out a five-year plan following graduation. The summer they graduated, they would get married, find great jobs, and become established in their careers. They planned to start their family after buying a home the fifth year.

Their plans changed when Kellie found herself pregnant with twins the second year of their marriage in spite of faithfully taking her birth control pills. Then Stan lost his job during a merger and had to start looking for another job to support his quickly growing but not intentionally planned family.

The stress of the unknown was extremely difficult on both of them. Kellie had to take early maternity leave because of preterm labor. They each went individually to God and began to inquire about their plans.

Stan said, "Kellie, I have a confession. I think our plans were good, but they were not God's plans."

Kellie agreed and said, "I think we need to give all our plans to God and let Him show us the plan He had for us."

As they gave up their own desires, God began to bring about His blessing for their new family. As they moved forward, allowing God to direct their path, they found their greatest opportunity in the biggest challenge they had ever faced.

*Lord, speak to me and show me the plans
You have for me today. Amen.*

This Christmas, God Wants You to Know. . .

What Love Would Do

Let love be genuine. Abhor what is evil; hold fast to what is good. Love one another with brotherly affection. Outdo one another in showing honor. Do not be slothful in zeal, be fervent in spirit, serve the Lord.
ROMANS 12:9–11 ESV

A few months before Christmas, Tim found himself thrust into leadership, responsible for a staff that needed a boost. And once again he challenged himself with determination to love them—no matter what challenges he faced, what obstacles he had to overcome, or what unrealistic deadlines he had to meet. He was determined to be honest and open and press in to discover the heartbeat of this team.

Tim knew that teams want to be celebrated and appreciated. He realized most people want an opportunity to develop their gifts and talents in an environment of trust. He had learned to lead with love—something many in the workplace did not expect from a new boss. Whenever he had challenges with individual employees, he asked himself, "What would love do?"

Tim remained determined to look at his new staff through God's eyes. *What would God say to them?* he thought. He decided He would say, "I love you. I trust you. I want you to succeed. Let's do this together." By Christmas Eve, they learned to thrive through simple acts of kindness—words of encouragement, cheer, applause, compassion, and loving correction.

Help me to see people through Your eyes of love and respond to them in the way that You would. Amen.

This Christmas, God Wants You to Know. . .

HOW TO EXTEND FORGIVENESS

Create in me a clean heart, O God, and renew a steadfast spirit within me. Do not cast me away from Your presence, and do not take Your Holy Spirit from me. Restore to me the joy of Your salvation, and uphold me by Your generous Spirit.

PSALM 51:10–12 NKJV

Mary and Brooke had been close for years. When they married, their husbands became friends, and eventually they began to raise their children together. One weekend the four of them went on a road trip without the kids. They had agreed they would return home at a specific time, but Mary and her husband went to see family and didn't come back on schedule.

Brooke and her husband waited for more than six hours, texting and calling them, trying to reach them to no avail. When Mary and her husband returned, she refused to take responsibility for the selfish delay. Brooke didn't speak to Mary the entire drive home, after giving her a piece of her mind. A wall went up in Brooke's heart. The two men tried to help their wives mend the relationship, but Brooke was done. The two families went their separate ways. Eight years passed before the two women spoke again. Because Brooke didn't understand fully God's forgiveness and love, she couldn't offer it to anyone else who really needed it.

Father, show me how to extend forgiveness to others just as You've given it to me. Amen.

This Christmas, God Wants You to Know. . .

HE WILL GIVE YOU THE DESIRES
OF YOUR HEART

Delight yourself also in the LORD,
and He shall give you the desires of your heart.
PSALM 37:4 NKJV

Candy loved babies. In grocery stores and coffee shops, they mesmerized her, even as a little girl. She mothered both her younger sisters, always ready and willing to help her mother with the babies. She was thankful when God blessed her with two beautiful boys of her own. As they grew up and moved away, her desire to nurture little ones remained.

So she waited and continued to ask God about this desire deep within her heart. Her husband suggested she volunteer at the local hospital and become a "cuddler" to newborns and infants in the neonatal ICU. Even with a full-time job, she was able to work a four-hour shift each week in the NICU.

Each week she had the opportunity to spend time with critically ill infants. She cared for them, comforted them, and prayed for God to make Himself known to them at an early age and to heal them. The nurses took notice of her gift to comfort and nurture even the sickest little ones. Some said, "She has the touch!" Others mentioned that peace fell over the whole room when she walked in. Even the tiniest ones that she was not allowed to hold seemed to respond to her voice or her touch.

As I delight myself in You,
may the desires of my heart be realized. Amen.

This Christmas, God Wants You to Know...

YOU HAVE TO LET GO OF THE OLD TO EXPERIENCE THE NEW

"For I am about to do something new. See, I have already begun!
Do you not see it? I will make a pathway through the wilderness.
I will create rivers in the dry wasteland."

ISAIAH 43:19 NLT

When family came to town, especially during the holidays, one of their favorite places to go was the gelato shop. As soon as Doug's niece and nephew arrived, he took the kids down to the gelato shop. His daughter, Laura, with her two cousins each took turns sampling the different flavors.

Doug wasn't quite sure why Laura even bothered to sample the other kinds of ice cream. She always came away with the dark-chocolate flavor. As they sat down to enjoy their bowls, he looked quizzically at his chocolate-loving daughter's bowl now filled with a swirly red peppermint-and-vanilla mix. "What is that?" he teased her. "No chocolate?"

"Dad, I decided to try something new. We had a lesson last Wednesday night at church about God doing new things in us. I learned that when we get set in our old ways and refuse to try something new, we might miss something God has for us. I am going to try something new every week and see how that goes."

"What do you think about this flavor?" he asked.

"I still like chocolate, but I like this one, too," Laura said.

I choose to let go of the old so I can experience
the new I have found in You. Amen.

This Christmas, God Wants You to Know. . .

YOU HAVE GIFTS TO GIVE

Do not neglect to do good and to share what you have,
for such sacrifices are pleasing to God.
HEBREWS 13:16 ESV

Giving gifts gets so old," Tara told her girlfriend Sheila. "I hate going to the store, looking at things, and trying to figure out what someone would or wouldn't like. My nieces and nephews always know in advance what they're going to get from me. My mother always says she doesn't want anything, but I always try to find something for her."

Sheila smiled. "Tara, you are a gift to me every single day. It's not just about wrapping a present and giving something tangible. Your smile, your heart to see others experience joy, and your brutal honesty that helps me tell myself the truth about things are all gifts you give me and I cherish every day."

"I guess you're right. I shouldn't stress over the gift giving each Christmas but be more concerned about the gifts and talents God has put within me and whether I am using them. I know it's important to sow into the lives of others with the spiritual gifts He's given. Maybe I've been looking at this all wrong. I think this year I will ask God what gifts He wants me to share with my family and how I can present them to each one in honor of Him."

Lord, show me how You want me to use my abilities
or talents to benefit others. Amen.

This Christmas, God Wants You to Know...

THANKFULNESS HAS MANY BENEFITS

Do all things without complaining and disputing,
that you may become blameless and harmless, children of God
without fault in the midst of a crooked and perverse generation,
among whom you shine as lights in the world.
PHILIPPIANS 2:14–15 NKJV

*A*nyone can be thankful when things are going well," Celia remarked to her brother, Brody. "It's when you're facing painful circumstances or difficult life challenges that remembering to express thankfulness can be hard." Celia had spent the last hour listening to him mumble and complain about little things in his life that weren't going quite right.

"I've met some remarkable people who have discovered how to be thankful no matter what. I've watched people suffer deep loss, and their thankful hearts continue. They have experienced the death of a loved one, the unexpected end of a long career, financial setbacks, and loss of health—all the time they're still expressing thanks to God."

"How do they do that?" Brody asked.

"When we can take our eyes off what we don't have, we can be thankful for all the good God has done," Celia replied. "Thanksgiving keeps us from getting stuck in a negative cycle of becoming bitter and cynical. They know what I am still learning: thankfulness for where you are helps you in the midst of whatever challenge is in front of you."

Lord, develop a heart of thankfulness in me. Amen.

This Christmas, God Wants You to Know. . .

PEACE ON EARTH

For God in all his fullness was pleased to live in Christ,
and through him God reconciled everything to himself.
He made peace with everything in heaven and on earth
by means of Christ's blood on the cross.
COLOSSIANS 1:19–20 NLT

Adrianna work up early Christmas morning. She slipped over to the sliding-glass door and peered through the curtains for a glimpse of the backyard filled with fresh snow. The blanket of white seemed to speak peace and tranquility to her soul. She saw a group of young deer emerge from the hedge of trees. They seemed to know that she was there behind the curtain. They watched her closely as they slipped up to the sidewalk that went out from the porch, looking for the corn that her husband usually left for them.

Suddenly she felt her still-sleepy four-year-old standing next to her. She placed her finger over her lips and then motioned for him to look out at the deer. She sat down on the floor and pulled him into her lap as they continued to experience the view together.

She breathed in a sweet, deep peace. All was quiet; all was calm. It was as if the world stopped and she thought this still and quiet moment with God was all she might ever need. Her soul reached out to God to take a drink of His peace, His strength.

Thank You, Lord, for Your peace and strength. Amen.

This Christmas, God Wants You to Know. . .

YOUR HURT CAN HELP OTHERS

Jesus said, "Come follow me, and I will make you fish for people."
MATTHEW 4:19 NCV

One Christmas break Jeremy, Don, and Dustin took a group of teenagers on a ski trip. Each man drove one of the vans packed full of kids and a few parents. Ten hours into the trip, the guys, who barely knew one another, began to share their lives over the handheld walkie-talkies they had brought along. Don, a grandfather and much older than the other two, kept Jeremy and Dustin awake with their coffee and his endless stories that lasted throughout the night.

Through their late-night talks, Jeremy and Dustin learned about Don's life. He shared his heart for unsaved loved ones, the challenges of raising a blended family, and the painful hole in his heart from losing a child to a tragic accident.

His willingness to share his own hurts with these younger men gave them hope. Jeremy was navigating an extremely difficult divorce, and Dustin was trusting God for his own parents to be saved.

Once they arrived at the ski resort and got some much-needed sleep, Jeremy told Don, "You've built some bridges for me. Before you shared your life, I was afraid to cross some difficult places in my life. Now I know that I can make it to the other side."

Lord, help me to be willing to share my hurts
as You lead me so that I can help others. Amen.

This Christmas, God Wants You to Know. . .

HOW BIG HIS LOVE IS FOR YOU

For God so loved the world that he gave his one and only Son,
that whoever believes in him shall not perish but have eternal life.
JOHN 3:16 NIV

Jason and Trista married young and started their family right away. Their first child was their entire world. When Mason was born, the love Jason felt for his son was so much greater than he imagined it would be.

When Trista said she was ready for another baby, he admitted his fear of not loving his second child as much as he did his first. *There is just so much love in my heart now,* he thought, *if I experience more, it's like my heart could explode.*

Trista went into labor on Christmas Eve, and their second son was born. Jason took his newborn baby into his arms and felt a powerful love grow immediately for this child. "It's like I grew another space in my heart to hold the love I have for this baby. It's hard to explain, but it wasn't there before," he told Trista.

Trista smiled. "It's hard to put into words," he continued. "I always wondered how God could love all of His children like the Bible says He does. Today, this baby of ours born on Christmas Eve helps me understand on a small scale just how big His love is for me."

Father, Your love is amazing.
No matter what comes my way—I will never doubt
Your unconditional love for me. Amen.

This Christmas, God Wants You to Know. . .

LIFE IS SELDOM PICTURE PERFECT

"I told you these things so that you can have peace in me.
In this world you will have trouble, but be brave!
I have defeated the world."
JOHN 16:33 NCV

*W*ith four children under the age of eight, it proved impossible to have professional portraits taken that Sarah was proud of. In years past, someone was crying, someone wasn't looking at the camera, and most of the time Sarah was so frazzled, her smile was plastered to her face.

She texted her husband and told him she just didn't want to do the family portraits this year. It was a big tradition with his family to exchange family portraits, and she knew his mother would be very disappointed. "It's okay," James offered, trying to be supportive. Then he had an idea. "What if we didn't make it a big deal, dressed the kids in jeans, and went out to the old farm. I think the big red barn still has some paint on it, and we could get some shot in front of it.

"We could take a picnic lunch and make it a relaxed family outing. I could get my photographer to come and take some shots for us with both of us in the photo." Sarah and James did just that. They made memories together that day, and the pictures turned out to be the best their family had ever taken.

Life happens sometimes, and I can't change it or control it.
Help me to be flexible with the less-than-perfect things. Amen.

This Christmas, God Wants You to Know. . .

His Word Will Light Your Way

Your word is a lamp for my feet, a light on my path.
PSALM 119:105 NIV

Since her husband died six years ago, Carla lived with her youngest daughter and her family. They had recently moved into a larger home with a double master so she would be more comfortable. She often woke up in the middle of the night and couldn't go back to sleep.

One night, she tried to slip quietly downstairs and into the kitchen to get some warm milk to help her sleep. She avoided turning on the lights in hopes of not disturbing the rest of the family. As she reached the main floor and walked through the living room toward the kitchen, she stumbled in the dark when her left food collided with the corner of the couch leg. The next morning her foot was swollen and bruised. She thought maybe a couple of her toes were broken.

Navigating a path in the dark is a snapshot of your life lived without the wisdom and knowledge available to you through relationship with God and His Word. Just like the furniture Carla ran into in her path in the dark, there are things that can litter your spiritual path. When you allow God's Word to penetrate your heart, it shines brightly ahead so that you are able to avoid the obstacles along your path.

Lord, remind me to keep the light of Your Word shining brightly on the road You have chosen for me today. Amen.

This Christmas, God Wants You to Know. . .

YOU ARE HIS CHILD

Yet to all who did receive him, to those who believed in his name,
he gave the right to become children of God—children born
not of natural descent, nor of human decision
or a husband's will, but born of God.
JOHN 1:12–13 NIV

Eighteen-month-old Marcus was content in his aunt Robyn's lap as they sat at the dining room table Christmas Eve. Erin, the baby's mother, snapped a photo of the two of them. Later that night several family members gathered around Erin's laptop to view the photographs she'd taken that day.

"Robyn, come over here," her mother-in-law, Tina, called. "You've got to see photo of you and Marcus. Even though he's not blood related, he could easily pass as your own child. He looks so much like you."

Robyn smiled. It was true. People often mistook Marcus as her child when she went shopping with Erin. "I love that people think he's mine. He's such a beautiful child, and I love that people see a strong family resemblance."

"I think God does that for us to demonstrate how once we become His child, there should be a strong family resemblance," Tina said. "We begin to look like Him, the more we discover who we are in Him. He wants our choices, decisions, and even our words to mirror His plan and purpose for our lives."

Father, I want to look and act like You.
Help me to demonstrate who You are in the actions
and decisions in my life each day. Amen.

This Christmas, God Wants You to Know. . .

HE WILL NEVER WITHHOLD ANYTHING GOOD FROM YOU

For the LORD God is a sun and shield; the LORD will give grace and glory; no good thing will He withhold from those who walk uprightly.
PSALM 84:11 NKJV

"Sometimes the things we want aren't good for us," Lisa explained to her thirteen-year-old daughter, Andrea.

"I know," Andrea replied. "It's just so difficult for me to watch my friends eat whatever they want during all the Christmas parties and stuff, knowing I can't have those things because of the diabetes."

"I know it's hard, but you have to do things differently," Lisa encouraged.

"I've learned that it doesn't benefit me either way. I usually don't feel well after I eat sweets. The immediate satisfaction just isn't worth it in the long run. . . but it's still tempting sometimes."

"There have been a lot of times in my life where I asked God for something that I was certain would be good for me or for our family, and He didn't make a way for that particular thing to happen," Lisa said. "At first I thought He was withholding something from me that would be good; but as I've watched how He works in my life, I've discovered that those things He withheld weren't good for me—even when they were good for other people."

I trust You. However You answer my prayers—
I believe You give me everything good. Amen.

This Christmas, God Wants You to Know...

ENCOURAGEMENT BUILDS FAITH

Worry is a heavy load, but a kind word cheers you up.
PROVERBS 12:25 NCV

Megan's day was filled with lots of work on several projects and meetings that were scheduled too close together. She finally was able to escape a little after five o'clock and rush home to change clothes for her niece Piper's dance recital. As Megan drove, she wondered what it would be like. It was her niece's third recital in a year but the first Megan was able to make.

She arrived with just a few minutes to spare before the curtain opened. She found her seat next to her brother, Alan, and sat down. As each person performed, the crowd was amazingly gracious. "I love how everyone cheered and applauded the dancers, especially the little ones," Megan whispered to Alan.

"Yes," Alan replied, "even though they made mistakes and sometimes aren't sure what to do next. Even the instructors and teammates encourage each other." Then he smiled a quirky smile and said, "As Christians we can take a lesson from these little ones. We need to do a better job of cheering on other believers, especially those who are new in the faith. Instead of being critical because they don't have it right, we should do a lot more applauding."

Megan smiled. *He has a point,* she thought, as she settled in to watch Piper's first dance.

I want to build others up and encourage them. Remind me
to applaud others as they grow in their faith. Amen.

This Christmas, God Wants You to Know. . .

It's Important to Prepare

Go watch the ants, you lazy person. Watch what they do and be wise. Ants have no commander, no leader or ruler, but they store up food in the summer and gather their supplies at harvest.
Proverbs 6:6–8 ncv

Christmas started early at the Johnson home. The Christmas lights went up throughout the yard usually a week or so before Thanksgiving. The day after Thanksgiving, the tree was chosen and placed in the living room, and all the children who lived close enough came over to help Mom trim the tree while Dad set out the Nativity scene, ran garland around the fireplace mantle, and hung the children's and grandchildren's stockings.

There was so much preparation that went into the big week of organizing and planning before Christmas. Dad carried boxes and boxes out of the attic weeks in advance. There was the cleaning and rearranging that went on all over the house as well as cookies—all different kinds—baked ahead, boxed, and frozen to give as gifts for friends. Mom always took a box or two to all the Christmas festivities throughout the month of December.

If you asked the Johnsons about the elaborate preparations, they would each tell you that preparing for Christmas reminded the entire family of how important it is to prepare and keep our hearts and homes for Jesus to live in us and through us.

Lord, let Christmas forever remind me to prepare and keep my heart for You. Amen.

This Christmas, God Wants You to Know. . .

IT'S ALL ABOUT THE LITTLE MOMENTS ALONG THE WAY

Nothing bad will happen to you; no disaster will come to your home.
He has put his angels in charge of you to watch over you
wherever you go. They will catch you in their hands
so that you will not hit your foot on a rock.
PSALM 91:10–12 NCV

Seven hours in the car with two toddlers in the backseat is not my idea of fun," Richard complained to his wife, Zoe.

"I know you're tired after all the long hours you've put in at work to get your project done before our Christmas vacation," Zoe replied. "We live life in fast-forward, and I'd like to enjoy the little stops along the way as we drive down south to see your family."

"Okay," Richard replied. "I'll feel better after I get some sleep tonight."

The next morning as he loaded the car, he had higher hopes for the family adventure. After two pretty calm hours in the car, and two hours at a petting zoo, Zoe and Richard were both enjoying the opportunity for adult conversation as the girls slept in their booster seats in the back of their Tahoe.

Don't let your focus be only on the destination. While it's nice to know where you're going, God desires for you to enjoy the little moments in between here and there.

I choose today to celebrate the little things You are doing in me
and through me as I move closer to my destiny. Amen.

This Christmas, God Wants You to Know. . .

IT'S BETTER FROM HIS PERSPECTIVE

For everyone who has been born of God overcomes the world.
And this is the victory that has overcome the world—our faith.
1 JOHN 5:4 ESV

Christina was cleaning the house in preparation for Christmas when she noticed what looked like an art portfolio sticking out of the top of the recycle trash can in the garage. She carried it into the kitchen, where the artist, Michelle, was eating breakfast.

"Honey, I found your art portfolio with all your beautiful artwork in the recycle bin. Why would you throw all your hard work away? What's up?" Christina asked.

"Oh, Mom," Michelle replied in frustration. "Just leave it there. It's just schoolwork. It's not very good. I don't want to keep it."

Christina opened the portfolio to find some stunning pieces created by her daughter's hand. "These are really good. I don't want you to throw them away."

"You're my mom," Michelle snapped. "You're supposed to say that."

"A few of these really speak to me," Christina pressed. "Could I at least frame a few for my office?"

"Really?" Michelle asked. "I guess, if you really believe they're good. Okay."

Sometimes you may not think what you have to offer is good enough, when in fact God sees your talent from His perspective—beautiful and ready for display.

I want to see myself from Your perspective.
Show me what You see in me. Amen.

This Christmas, God Wants You to Know. . .

HEAVEN IS A REAL PLACE

The Lord himself will come down from heaven with
a loud command, with the voice of the archangel,
and with the trumpet call of God.
And those who have died believing in Christ will rise first.
1 THESSALONIANS 4:16 NCV

*M*ost people find a cemetery an odd thing for someone to say they enjoy, but it seemed very comfortable for Hannah. Her paternal grandfather's side of the family had a cemetery that she had visited when she was a child. She loved to steal quiet moments away, sitting on the old, dirty pews inside the small church built in the late 1800s that still stood on the property where her ancestors had worshipped.

Her father's brother was buried just outside the church—a man she had never met. The family didn't talk about him much, but she knew what he looked like because there was a photograph of him set with the stone. Having lost a grandmother she was extremely close to while she was still a child, she knew the people weren't really there anyway.

She loved to think of heaven and all the people who would greet her when she got there. She imagined many of those whose names she read in the family cemetery would be there. She believed they would know her and she would know them.

Heaven is a real place. Help me to understand
that my time here on earth is just the beginning
of the eternity I will share with You. Amen.

This Christmas, God Wants You to Know. . .

HE WANTS TO TEACH YOU

This is what we speak, not in words taught us by human wisdom but in words taught by the Spirit, explaining spiritual realities with Spirit-taught words. The person without the Spirit does not accept the things that come from the Spirit of God but considers them foolishness, and cannot understand them because they are discerned only through the Spirit.
1 CORINTHIANS 2:13–14 NIV

A. W. Tozer, speaking to his generation, said, "We are raising a generation that wants to feel right rather than live right." Each person must learn what is right and what is wrong in order to live according to God's purpose and plan. The Bible, God's Word, is full of life lessons He wants to teach you. He has much He wants to teach you this Christmas.

The book of Proverbs is a great place to begin. Proverbs 1:5 says, "A wise man will hear and increase learning. And a man of understanding will attain wise counsel" (NKJV). The book of Proverbs provides the greatest counsel ever received. It gives you a mental picture of what is important for you to say and do to experience life in Christ.

As you allow Him to teach you, you will adapt your lifestyle to His authority and His ways. The road to the blessed life includes a pliable heart, where you are willing to hear and follow His instruction.

I desire to be teachable. I open my heart and receive instruction from You today. Amen.

This Christmas, God Wants You to Know. . .

THE HEALING POWER OF LAUGHTER

We were filled with laughter, and we sang for joy. And the other nations said, "What amazing things the LORD has done for them."
PSALM 126:2 NLT

LaDonna's mother, Cheryl, was very reserved. Her prim and proper personality often frustrated LaDonna—especially when it came to raising LaDonna's four boys. She was nervous when her parents said they wanted to join her family at their home in Colorado the week of Christmas. Her parents arrived just as the first heavy snow fell on their Colorado valley home.

The next morning LaDonna and Cheryl stood at the windows watching the boys with their dad and granddad in the snow. The boys had built an igloo that ran along the side of the garage. Dad and Granddad were like little kids; they got right down in the middle of it all—laughing and roughhousing.

LaDonna stepped back into the kitchen to put the tea-kettle back on the stove for a second round of hot choco-late when she heard the front door open and close. When she walked back into the living room, her mother was gone. She peered outside to see her mother on the ground laugh-ing with the boys, and *they were rolling her in the snow!*

E. E. Cummings said, "The most wasted of all days is one without laughter."

Help me not to take myself so seriously that I can't take a moment to experience the healing power of laughter. Amen.

This Christmas, God Wants You to Know. . .

HE DELIVERS JUSTICE

The LORD does what is right, and he loves justice,
so honest people will see his face.
PSALM 11:7 NCV

*M*allory hated injustice. She was quick to stand up for herself and others. Sometimes her compulsion to become the defense had placed her in some challenging circumstances, especially when her passion to stand up for what she thought was right missed the mark of God's timing and what He wanted to do in her life.

She often found herself apologizing for a misunderstanding or wishing she could take back words she'd spewed in a heated discussion. Over time, she began to realize things aren't always as they first seem. Her perception of reality could put her on the wrong side of a situation. Thankfully for Mallory, she had discovered God is merciful and gracious, and usually others are willing to forgive. She began to ask God how to respond to situations instead of taking things into her own hands.

If your desire is to bring glory to God, then your actions will reflect just that. He will help you respond in love and peace in the midst of a wrong done to you or to others. When you let Him deliver the justice, you can trust that the result is always right for the situation.

When I am faced with injustice,
Lord, give me Your perspective and help me
to respond in a way that pleases You. Amen.

This Christmas, God Wants You to Know. . .

EVERYONE NEEDS COMPASSION

When the Lord saw her, his heart overflowed with compassion.
"Don't cry!" he said. Then he walked over to the coffin
and touched it, and the bearers stopped. "Young man,"
he said, "I tell you, get up." Then the dead boy sat up and began to talk!
And Jesus gave him back to his mother.
LUKE 7:13–15 NLT

Jesus saw a funeral procession as He approached the village gate. The boy who had died was the only son of a widow, and many mourners from the village were with her. The Bible said He was overcome with compassion for the woman. His heart went out to her for what she was experiencing.

Then, Jesus did the unexpected—the miraculous. He offered her hope. He stopped the funeral procession and raised the young man from the dead. The world is full of loss. People experience the loss of loved ones. People struggle with lost hopes and dreams when expectations fall short. Broken promises can produce broken lives. Whatever the circumstance people are going through, they need a kind heart.

Jesus is your example. He reached out to those who had no one else. He heard those no one else wanted to acknowledge. He saw the invisible ones—those in society that others refused to see.

Lord, give me a heart like Yours so I can do whatever is necessary to help others when they are in need. Amen.

This Christmas, God Wants You to Know. . .

JESUS IS YOUR ADVOCATE

"Therefore whoever confesses Me before men, him I will also confess before My Father who is in heaven."
MATTHEW 10:32 NKJV

*L*iz wanted to run to her husband Ben's defense. After eight years of excellent service, a coworker accused him of something he didn't do. She wanted the truth to be known. The accuser was a trusted friend of Ben's boss, and his daughter was in their daughter's dance class.

"Liz, you seem more upset and angry about this than I am," Ben commented.

"Maybe I am," she replied. "I hate that someone is trying to ruin your reputation. I know you'd never do anything unethical or even put the company in a negative light."

"We have to wait," Ben repeatedly told her. "Jesus is my advocate in this situation. I don't believe I'm supposed to say anything to defend myself. We have to trust God."

As Christmas approached, it was difficult to see the accuser and his family at the staff Christmas party, their daughter's recital, and other places. Then slowly the truth began to come to light. Little pieces of truth erupted and caused questions in Ben's boss's mind. Then suddenly the truth was made known—not just to Ben's boss but to the whole department, and Ben was exonerated. The accuser apologized, asked for forgiveness, and Ben's reputation was restored.

Jesus, be my advocate in difficult matters. Help me to love others past the circumstances as You defend me. Amen.

This Christmas, God Wants You to Know. . .

WISDOM IS YOURS

*If any of you lacks wisdom, let him ask God, who gives generously
to all without reproach, and it will be given him.*
JAMES 1:5 ESV

"I wish I had known the things I know now, when I was
in my twenties having my children," Belinda commented to
her friend Molly as they wrapped Christmas gifts. "I would
have done so many things differently. I watch you and others
who waited until their mid-thirties to have children, and
you parent with such wisdom and understanding."

Molly smiled. "That's a sweet thing to say, but I don't
know that it has as much to do with age as it has to do with
knowing where the wisdom comes from."

Belinda looked at her, puzzled. "What do you mean?"

Molly continued. "I am learning to tap into God's
wisdom for my life—especially when it comes to my kids.
Wisdom is insight: seeing through the divine perspective
and knowing what to do. There have been many times I felt
a tug in my heart say, 'Don't do it that way; do it this way.' "

"I see what you're saying," Belinda acknowledged. "Most
of the time we want to do things quickly and move on.
Hearing God and responding in His wisdom takes patience
and effort. I need to put His wisdom to work in every area
of my life."

*Heavenly Father, help me be patient as I listen and receive
Your wisdom in every area for my life today. Amen.*

This Christmas, God Wants You to Know. . .

YOUR STORY CAN ENCOURAGE OTHERS

I will tell how you do what is right. I will tell about your
salvation all day long, even though it is more than I can tell.
I will come and tell about your powerful works, Lord GOD.
I will remind people that only you do what is right.
PSALM 71:15–16 NCV

A child of divorce, Vickie struggled with the emotional scars left in her heart early into adulthood. For years she stuffed the pain and pretended she was over it. But when her brother went through his own divorce after three children and fifteen years of marriage—something in Vickie broke as she tried to help her brother navigate the pain.

She looked for and found a certified grief-recovery specialist who helped her realize she'd never fully recovered from the hurts left from spending her teenage years without her father's influence. At the end of process, she found that she was finally free. With God's help she had given voice to the emotional statements that needed to be said to help her heal. She then shared her story with her brother and other friends—who chose to benefit from her experience.

Vickie found that if she was willing to open and share what God had done in her life, He then used it to help them navigate a difficulty in their own lives.

Many times in my life, Lord, You have helped me overcome.
Help me to share my story so that it may help
others find victory through You. Amen.

This Christmas, God Wants You to Know. . .

IT PLEASES HIM TO GIVE YOURSELF AWAY

So now faith, hope, and love abide, these three;
but the greatest of these is love.
1 CORINTHIANS 13:13 ESV

Something was different about Kate. Stephanie watched her closely from the passenger side of Kate's car as they drove toward the biggest and busiest mall in town. They had come a standstill several times in the last thirty minutes, trying to get to one store Kate needed to go to for a gift for her mother. "Thanks for coming with me, Steph," Kate quipped as she paused to let yet another driver go in front of her.

"You're welcome," Steph replied, crinkling her nose and forehead. "So what's up with all the nicey-nice? Normally you are yelling at drivers, honking, trying to keep them from cutting you off. You even gave that lady your parking place at the last store. I'm just trying to figure you out."

"Christmas this year reminded me God did not put me on the earth to serve myself. Sometimes I know I can be really selfish. I am trying to keep the thought that others should see Christ in me. God sent Jesus to the earth to give Himself away. If I prefer others and put them ahead of myself, then hopefully they will see Christ in me—not just at Christmas but all the time."

Help me, Lord, to see each opportunity You set before me
to give myself away to others—just as You did when
You sent Jesus that first Christmas Day. Amen.

This Christmas, God Wants You to Know. . .

THE HEART OF CHRISTMAS RESIDES WITHIN YOU

*To them God has chosen to make known among
the Gentiles the glorious riches of this mystery,
which is Christ in you, the hope of glory.*
COLOSSIANS 1:27 NIV

An angelic host came to celebrate the promise delivered in the form of a baby—a child that was God made flesh—born to give life to all who would receive Him. That first Christmas more than two thousand years ago hope was born for all.

Christmas today lends to an outward celebration—far from the real cause for celebration that brought a host of angels to earth to sing God's praises. The "sale" of Christmas begins each year months in advance with advertisements in every form of media. The shopping malls are decorated in lights calling you to the store where every business wants a piece of your Christmas celebration. Calendars fill up with family get-togethers and office parties, and Christmas songs play over the loudspeakers wherever you go. Coffee shops push their Christmas flavors, and Santas ring the bell, hoping for a generous donation this time of year.

This Christmas, God wants you to know the heart of Christmas is within you. Turn your heart to the original Christmas, and remember how the angels rejoiced in God's greatest gift ever given. Their example is a snapshot of the reason for celebration.

*When I think about Christmas, help me to look within my
own heart and experience the true reason to celebrate. Amen.*

This Christmas, God Wants You to Know. . .

It's Never Too Late for Another Chance

Listen! The LORD's arm is not too weak to save you,
nor is his ear too deaf to hear you call.
ISAIAH 59:1 NLT

Jonah wanted to do things his way—not God's. When he refused God's direction to go and preach to the people of Nineveh, his choice landed him in the belly of a big fish. When he finally realized the road he took wasn't the safest route, he asked God to save him.

Maybe, like Jonah, you thought you had a better plan. Perhaps you imagined your way would save God some time if you did things on your own, but then it didn't turn out quite like you imagined. Christmas is all about second chances; Jesus' birth was the beginning of God's plan for second chances for everyone.

Jonah found himself about to be a whale's dinner. He realized God was his only salvation. He repented, and God made the whale spit him out. Jonah realized God's way was the best way—and he went to Nineveh rejoicing and thanking God for another chance to do what God had asked him to do, ultimately fulfilling a purpose God had for his life.

If you feel like you've blown it, God is closer than you think. God doesn't keep count of wrongs but is ready to turn things around for you today.

I choose Your way today. Forgive me for doing things my way.
I let go of what I want and follow Your lead. Amen.

This Christmas, God Wants You to Know. . .

JESUS CAME TO GIVE YOU ABUNDANT LIFE

"The thief comes only to steal and kill and destroy.
I came that they may have life and have it abundantly."
JOHN 10:10 ESV

A baby changes everything," Trent said. "I want children, I really do. The hard part is knowing when."

His wife, Angela, sighed. "If we wait until everything is perfect, we may never have children."

Angela was ready for a child, but Trent wasn't sure. He knew it took a lot financially to raise a child. They agreed to pray together about God's timing in starting their family.

As Christmas approached, they began to receive gifts in the mail. "Look!" Angela exclaimed as she opened a package. She pulled a beautiful, hand-crocheted baby blanket from the box. Trent opened the little card that read, *When you're ready. . . Love, Aunt Lilly.*

Trent followed Angela into the guest bedroom, where she had laid all the Christmas gifts they'd received so far out on the bed. "Are all these gifts for a baby?" he asked.

"Yes," Angela smiled. "Every gift we've received so far has been for our baby—not yet conceived."

It looked like a baby shower had erupted on their guest bed. "I believe God is letting us know that He is going to provide all we need for our family. He has given us the answer. It's time to start our family."

I trust You, Lord, to provide all I need.
You are my source of abundant life today! Amen.

This Christmas, God Wants You to Know. . .

HE STARTS WITH THE IMPOSSIBLE

Now all glory to God, who is able, through his mighty power at work within us, to accomplish infinitely more than we might ask or think. Glory to him in the church and in Christ Jesus through all generations forever and ever! Amen.
EPHESIANS 3:20–21 NLT

At forty-three years old and with the responsibility of a family and a full-time job, Tanya just could not fathom going back to school to complete her bachelor's degree. Her employer was pushing for it and even willing to help pay for some of it. Surprisingly, her husband, Max, was fully supportive.

"You can do it," Max said. "The kids and I will help take up the slack."

"I don't know," Tanya wavered.

"Just pray about it. Whatever you decide, I'll support."

Christmas was coming up quickly, and Tanya felt the full weight of a busy schedule. After several weeks of prayer, she and Max had another conversation. "It just seems crazy—impossible, in fact, for me to go back to school, but I believe I'm supposed to do it," she said.

"Look back on our life," Max encouraged. "God often asked for the impossible. If it were easily attainable, we wouldn't need to use our faith. Everything we've done well, we've done by faith."

"You are right," she said. "I have peace in my heart and will trust God every step of the way."

Thank You for asking me to do what seems impossible and for the strength to achieve it by faith. Amen.

This Christmas, God Wants You to Know. . .

HE WANTS YOUR WHOLE HEART

For the word of God is living and powerful, and sharper than any
two-edged sword, piercing even to the division of soul and spirit,
and of joints and marrow, and is a discerner
of the thoughts and intents of the heart.
HEBREWS 4:12 NKJV

When paramedics arrive on the scene with a lifeless body, aside from checking for a pulse, they look to see if the injured person is breathing—they're looking for signs of life. It could be said that your soul is where your spirit breathes—your life. Physically, your heart is the most vital of all organs. It is brings the life-sustaining blood to every single cell in your body.

Often the word *heart* is used to describe the soul, or the mind, as the fountain where all thoughts, passions, desires, appetites, and affections flow from—the life source of our inner being or spirit. This is where our eternal spirit resides and where from our spirit man we can touch the presence of God.

God desires relationship. He wants to be connected to you. Everything you are spiritually, physically, emotionally, financially, and socially should fit into the heartbeat of the Father. When you give Him your whole heart, you connect with Him on such a level that your own heart beats in rhythm with Him, and your lifestyle reflects that bond.

Father, I want to share my life with You. Let my lifestyle
reflect a heart that beats in rhythm with You. Amen.

This Christmas, God Wants You to Know. . .

ETERNAL LIFE BEGINS THE MOMENT YOU BELIEVE

This is what God told us: God has given us eternal life,
and this life is in his Son. Whoever has the Son has life,
but whoever does not have the Son of God does not have life.
1 JOHN 5:11–12 NCV

*L*auren trudged through the snow out to the shop where her stepdad was working. She offered him the steaming-hot mug of coffee and then motioned for him to sit down with her on a bench positioned near the shop heater. "So, Dad, you've never told me your story," she pressed him.

Thankful for the warm liquid and a chance to sit down, Eddie sighed. "I don't talk about it, really. . . ." He paused. "But I guess I should tell you." He struggled to find his words as it began to snow outside the open shop doors. "I had a daughter close to your age—she drowned. Several years before I met your mother, I was still lost. Then, somewhere, between 'Why' and 'Where are You, God?' I found the Son of God."

Eddie continued, "I never sobered up so fast as when I saw Jesus standing in front of me. That instant, I gave my life to God, and I've been a new man ever since." He handed Lauren the cup of coffee that was now cold. "The minute I believed, I suddenly felt alive again."

God, You have given me eternal life.
I don't have to wait to go to heaven
but can experience Your life in me today. Amen.

This Christmas, God Wants You to Know. . .

BEFORE YOU LIVED A DAY HE IMAGINED YOU

For we are God's handiwork, created in Christ Jesus to do good works, which God prepared in advance for us to do.
EPHESIANS 2:10 NIV

When a child is conceived, God's masterpiece begins to take shape. Parents may have hopes of what that child might look like, and who he or she will become, but He alone knows the full potential within the little baby to become more than his or her parents could possibly imagine. His plan is already in motion to bring joy and goodness into the lives of others.

Before you ever lived a day, God imagined you. He knew you in His heart and mind before you ever came to be. He believed you to be extraordinary, beautiful, and good. He designed you for His pleasure—to see you serve Him in a specific way. He filled you with talents and gifts that only you possess. He placed you into relationships in the lives of others that only you can touch.

You are God's work! He has created you as His own masterpiece and given you everything you need to become an exquisite, unique part of eternity. Ask Him to show you the gifts and talents He has given you. He will lead you in the way He has purposed, but you must choose to follow Him.

Father, I desire to be pliable, shaped only by Your hand. Give me insight into all that You imagined, and show me how I fit into Your plan. Amen.

This Christmas, God Wants You to Know. . .

You Can Experience Reconciliation

*Since we have been made right with God by our faith,
we have peace with God. This happened through our Lord Jesus Christ.*
ROMANS 5:1 NCV

*T*ammy's wedding was the perfect opportunity for God to do a miracle in the family. More than twenty years ago, the family was fractured when her uncle Shane and aunt Sherry divorced. Aunt Sherry took her three girls and moved thousands of miles away. Tammy had only seen her cousins twice the whole time they were teenagers, and she wasn't sure but felt like the girls hadn't seen their dad very many more times than that.

But now everyone was grown and on their own, and Tammy had invited them all to the wedding in hopes of reconnecting the family. So far, everyone had RSVP'd. She wasn't expecting it to be perfect, but she hoped time together would build a bridge for repair to lost relationships.

Tammy's desire to see parts of her family reconnected is similar to God's desire to connect with His family. Through Jesus' sacrifice, death, burial, and resurrection, He built a bridge that offered all who were willing to accept Him a way to eternal life. He built a bridge that could reconcile God and His creation. Jesus points the way to all men to join God's family and become reconciled to Him.

*Heavenly Father, thank You for sending Jesus
to build a bridge of reconciliation for me.
I accept Your gift of eternal life. Amen.*

This Christmas, God Wants You to Know. . .

He Is the Greatest Gift Giver

Then the LORD God formed the man from the dust of the ground.
He breathed the breath of life into the man's nostrils,
and the man became a living person.
GENESIS 2:7 NLT

Abby pushed the stroller through the crowded mall, trying to finish up the last of her Christmas shopping as her baby girl slept. She tried to patiently wait her turn in a cramped novelty store when her eyes fell on a beautifully crafted figurine titled "Adam's First Breath." It demonstrated God's gift of life as He breathed into Adam's nostrils, symbolized by a small cloud going into Adam's face as he slept.

Abby had never seen anything like it. The beautiful piece of art captivated her heart, and immediately she began to think of God's goodness and love for her—His creation. *God is a giver, not a taker. He gave from His very own breath of life to create Adam,* she thought. She began to recount the stories in the Bible that evidenced His generous gifts to humanity.

She looked down at her daughter, still sleeping. She knew she could never deny God's existence or His gifts of goodness in her life with just one glimpse of her child. Just as she wanted to give precious gifts to her daughter, she knew God's heart was the same as hers—to give all of Himself for each of His children.

Of all the gifts I give and receive this Christmas, help me remember the greatest gifts always come from You. Amen.

Scripture Index